Motets for Two to Six Voices
Opus 1

Recent Researches in Music

A-R Editions publishes seven series of critical editions, spanning the history of Western music, American music, and oral traditions.

Recent Researches in the Music of the Middle Ages and Early Renaissance
    Charles M. Atkinson, general editor

Recent Researches in the Music of the Renaissance
    James Haar, general editor

Recent Researches in the Music of the Baroque Era
    Steven Saunders, general editor

Recent Researches in the Music of the Classical Era
    Neal Zaslaw, general editor

Recent Researches in the Music of the Nineteenth and Early Twentieth Centuries
    Rufus Hallmark, general editor

Recent Researches in American Music
    John M. Graziano, general editor

Recent Researches in the Oral Traditions of Music
    Philip V. Bohlman, general editor

Each edition in *Recent Researches* is devoted to works by a single composer or to a single genre. The content is chosen for its high quality and historical importance and is edited according to the scholarly standards that govern the making of all reliable editions.

For information on establishing a standing order to any of our series, or for editorial guidelines on submitting proposals, please contact:

A-R Editions, Inc.
Middleton, Wisconsin

800 736-0070 (North American book orders)
608 836-9000 (phone)
608 831-8200 (fax)
http://www.areditions.com

Recent Researches in the Music of the Baroque Era, 173

Bonifazio Graziani

Motets for Two to Six Voices Opus 1

Edited by Lars Berglund

A-R Editions, Inc.
Middleton, Wisconsin

A-R Editions, Inc., Middleton, Wisconsin
© 2011 by A-R Editions, Inc.

All rights reserved. No part of this book may be reproduced
or transmitted in any form by any electronic or mechanical
means (including photocopying, recording, or information
storage and retrieval) without permission in writing from
the publisher.

The purchase of this edition does not convey the right to
perform it in public, nor to make a recording of it for any
purpose. Such permission must be obtained in advance
from the publisher.

A-R Editions is pleased to support scholars and performers
in their use of *Recent Researches* material for study or performance. Subscribers to any of the *Recent Researches* series,
as well as patrons of subscribing institutions, are invited to
apply for information about our "Copyright Sharing Policy."

Printed in the United States of America

ISBN 978-0-89579-707-0
ISSN 0484-0828

♾ The paper used in this publication meets the minimum
requirements of the American National Standard for
Information Sciences—Permanence of Paper for Printed
Library Materials, ANSI Z39.48-1992.

Contents

Acknowledgments   vi

Introduction   vii
  Biography   vii
  Graziani's Opus 1 and the Holy Year of 1650   vii
  Singers and Musicians at the Church of the Gesù   viii
  The Music   viii
  Performance   ix
  Notes   ix

Texts and Translations, *Edited and Translated by Peter Sjökvist*   xi

Plates   xvi

Motets for Two to Six Voices, Opus 1
  (All numbers are with basso continuo)

  Dedication   2
    1. Hic est panis *(CC)*   3
    2. Ludite, canite *(CC)*   11
    3. Omnes gentes *(CC)*   20
    4. Amen dico vobis *(CB)*   26
    5. Domine, ne in furore tuo *(CCB)*   30
    6. Ad mensam dulcissimi *(CCT)*   39
    7. Haec est vera fraternitas *(CCB)*   47
    8. O Jesu, fili Mariae *(CCC)*   55
    9. Aperi mihi *(ATB)*   64
    10. Salve, o dulce amoris *(CAT)*   69
    11. Veni electa mea *(CCC)*   77
    12. Surge, veni *(CCT)*   85
    13. Rex magne caelitum *(CCB)*   98
    14. Anima nostra *(CCTB)*   108
    15. Quid est hoc *(CCAB)*   117
    16. O principes *(CCATB)*   127
    17. Venite gentes *(CCATB)*   144
    18. Justus ut palma *(CCCATB)*   154

Critical Report   167
  Source   167
  Editorial Methods   167
  Critical Notes   168

Acknowledgments

The preparation of this edition was made possible thanks to a project grant from the Swedish Research Council. I extend my gratitude to the Museo internazionale e biblioteca della musica di Bologna for microfilms of the 1650 Graziani edition and for the permission to publish this edition. My thanks go also to the A-R Editions staff for their assistance. My warm appreciation goes to Dr. Peter Sjökvist, who edited and translated the Latin texts; to my collegues at the Department of Musicology at Uppsala University; and to Dr. habil. Peter Wollny at the Bach-Archiv, Leipzig, for help and advice.

Introduction

Concerted liturgical church music, and especially small-scale motets and concertos, were central genres in Western music in the mid-seventeenth century. Such pieces made up the core of daily and weekly musical practices both at Roman Catholic church services and at princely and royal court chapels, in Catholic as well as in Lutheran regions. The most admired and emulated music was composed by Italian musicians, and from sometime around 1650 it appears as if the Roman composers took the lead. One of the most important figures in this process was the *maestro di cappella* of the Jesuit Church of the Gesù, Bonifazio Graziani.

Biography

Bonifazio Graziani (1604/5–1664) was raised in Marino, a small town located in the Alban hills, some thirty kilometers south of Rome. Little is known of his early years, though it seems that he obtained musical education of some kind and received his orders in Marino. In the same town, in the very same period, Giacomo Carissimi was born and raised. The two of them must have been acquainted, and they were later to make very similar musical careers at Jesuit institutions in Rome.

Graziani seems to have stayed in Marino and in the nearby town Frascati until the 1640s, possibly active both as a priest and as a church organist.[1] In 1646 he is recorded as a *canonicus vicarius* and secretary to the abbot in Marino. Later that year he left for Rome, where he took up the position as *maestro di cappella* at the Jesuit Pontifical Roman Seminary and the church connected with it, Il Gesù, a position he was to retain for the remainder of his life.

Few biographical data from Graziani's eighteen years in Rome have come down to us. He took up residence in the seminary, but according to a document in the archive of the seminary he was later allowed to move to an outside residence in order to be able to compose undisturbed.[2] During his lifetime Graziani published nine printed collections of music, not counting the many reissues. The prints include liturgical music of different types: solo motets as well as motets for two to six voices, psalms, litanies, responsories, etc. His music was apparently much in demand. After Graziani's death, his brother and nephew made sure to immediately obtain the rights from Pope Alexander VII to publish his compositions.[3] Between 1665 and 1678 they published at least fourteen posthumous collections of music by Graziani.

Graziani's greatest successes were apparently his collections of solo motets (opp. 3, 6, 8, 10, and 16). However, his first collection of multiple-voiced motets, *Motetti a due, tre, quattro, cinque, e sei voci*, opus 1 (1650) seems to have been equally successful. It was reprinted first in Antwerp in 1652, then once again in Rome in 1654. Moreover, among the numerous works by Graziani that were disseminated in manuscripts throughout Europe—there are sources in at least twenty-six libraries, in at least eight countries—there is a large share of motets from opus 1.[4]

The impact of Graziani's motets north of the Alps during the 1650s and 1660s can hardly be overestimated. Judging from preserved emulations by contemporary composers, he was the most frequently imitated of all Italian composers of liturgical music during that time, outnumbering even Giacomo Carissimi.

Graziani's Opus 1 and the Holy Year of 1650

The year 1650 was memorable in Rome, as well as in Graziani's career. According to a long tradition this year was declared an *anno santissimo*, a most holy year, by Pope Innocent X, which meant that thousands of pilgrims flocked to the eternal city, enticed by the extraordinary offer of indulgences. It also gave reason for massive ventures of building and decorating in the city, as well as splendid ceremonies and festive arrangements of different kinds, all in an effort to display the grandeur of Rome.[5]

For Graziani, as a musician and composer, the festivities resulted in many important tasks and commissions. In addition to the regular weekly services, he was responsible for the musical ornamentation of several solemn rituals and celebrations. The feast of the Circumcision, on January 1, was also the day of the name-giving of Jesus, and therefore an important day for Il Gesù, dedicated as it was to the name of Jesus. The same goes for the feast of Corpus Christi, on the Thursday after Trinity Sunday. Furthermore, great celebrations were held on the feast days of the Jesuit saints, Ignatius Loyola (July 31), Francis Borgia (September 30), and Francis Xavier (December 2). For all these occasions Graziani composed and performed solemn large-scale music for multiple choirs—four to six *cori spezzati* seem to have been standard at such feasts.[6] However, very few examples of such compositions by Graziani have survived.[7]

Another important occasion for solemn music at Il Gesù was during the Forty Hours' Devotion (Quarant' Ore), late in February 1650. The tradition of displaying the Sacrament during forty hours with a magnificent *apparato,* or theatrical set, was old, but it reached something of a peak this year, with the representation of the Temple of Solomon in Il Gesù.[8] This particular *apparato* was much admired and was reported in the *avvisi* as well as in contemporary reports of the holy year.[9] Music appears to have accompanied the solemn presentation, which was attended by Pope Innocent X, the college cardinals, and a large number of other prominent guests.[10] It seems likely that Graziani used some of the motets with Eucharistic texts from his opus 1 (see, e.g., nos. 1, 6, and 10) for such an occasion.

In April, Graziani had one of his most honorable commissions: to compose and perform oratorio music for the Oratory of the Most Holy Crucifix near the church of San Marcello. The archconfraternity of the Most Holy Crucifix arranged music at this oratory each year during Lent. It was the only place in Rome where oratorios in Latin were presented, and it must be considered one of the most important musical institutions in the city.[11]

During the holy year of 1650, it was decided that oratorios should be performed during all five consecutive Fridays of Lent. Five different musicians were selected for the task, by five different patrons, all members of the archconfraternity.[12] Among the five *maestri di cappella* engaged during 1650 were Loreto Vittorio and Giacomo Carissimi. For the fifth and last oratorio gathering, the patron, Cardinal Gaspare Mattei, chose Graziani as composer and leader. It seems most likely that the two Latin oratorios preserved in a manuscript in Bologna, *Adam* and *Filii prodigi,* are the works that were performed on this occasion.[13]

It is explicitly stated on the title page of the print that the publication of Graziani's first collection of motets was connected with the holy year (see plate 1). The collection may in this sense be considered part of the extraordinary ornamentation and manifestation of the eternal city during the *anno santissimo*. Still, the reasons for its publication were arguably manifold. One was probably the ambition to manifest the musical splendor of the Jesuit seminar and the church: Graziani's position is also stated on the title page. The fact that his music was considered a pride of the church is clear from the entry in the church records that note his death: "Today June 15 died in Marino Signor Bonifazio Graziani, who left great ecclesiastical works to this church."[14] However, another important reason was undoubtedly commercial: the anxiety of Graziani's heirs to secure the publishing rights in 1664 indicates that the publication of musical prints could be a profitable affair.

The motets in Graziani's opus 1 were probably composed during the second half of the 1640s and were primarily intended for the liturgical needs of Il Gesù. There were numerous occasions for the performance of motets of this kind in the church rituals. The obvious one was for the mass services on Sundays and feast days, during which at least two different motets substituted for liturgical elements of the proper of the mass, and not the least at the vespers, where motets similarly could substitute for the antiphons. The performance of one motet was also prescribed at the Saturday Litany.[15]

Some of the works in Graziani's opus 1 are settings of mystical devotional texts (such as "Hic est panis" and "Ad mensam dulcissimi"). These are clearly intended for the Communion and for the Elevation of the Host.

Moreover, there were several occasions to perform motets such as those under discussion here outside the regular services of Il Gesù. The "Avvisi per il M. di Capella" of the Pontifical Roman Seminary states that the *maestro* was supposed to practice part-singing with the *alumni* every day after lunch. Graziani may have used some of the vocally less demanding motets for such pedagogical purposes. Motets could also be performed at different non-liturgical devotional gatherings at the Casa Professa, the Jesuit headquarters, adjacent to the church. Furthermore, as we have seen, motets could be used at ceremonies such as the Forty Hours' Devotion and similar devotional festivities.

Singers and Musicians at the Church of the Gesù

Two categories of singers were engaged at Il Gesù. First, the seminary employed four full-time singers.[16] All were of course male singers, most likely not castratos, but soprano and alto falsettos, along with a tenor and a bass. In addition to these, it is clear from the church records that Graziani regularly engaged two or three papal singers, members of the Sistine Chapel. Among these were sopranos, contraltos, and a tenor, Martino Lamotta. It seems likely that these prominent singers were engaged to sing the rather demanding parts that are found in many of Graziani's motets.

Some of the other musicians active at Il Gesù are also known by name. The most important is the organist appearing in the payroll around the time of Graziani's opus 1: from December 1649 until March 1651 this position was filled by a very young Vincenzo Albrici—before this he had been active as an organist at the Oratorian church Santa Maria in Vallicella (also known as "Chiesa Nuova").[17] After giving up his post at Il Gesù he was to travel as far north as Stockholm, as a prominent member of the Italian troupe of singers and musicians engaged at the court of Queen Christina of Sweden. During the 1660s he was kapellmeister at the electoral court of Saxony in Dresden. Albrici was an extremely important person for the dissemination of the Roman motet style north of the Alps, and there can be no doubt that one of his main influences was Graziani.[18]

The Music

The eighteen motets in Graziani's opus 1 reflect a remarkably modern stance of ecclesiastical compositional practice, which is revealed on different levels. One such trait is the combination of compound structure and stylistic plurality within single works. The motets present a combination of free and inventive concertato writing, spiced with aria and recitative inflections. In addition, there are independent aria sections, as well as brief passages in *stile recitativo*.

Characteristic, and modern, is also the distinctly harmonically founded conception of Graziani's music: harmonic schemes and patterns pre-structure much of his composition. In this respect, he differs from contemporaries such as Francesco Foggia and Giacomo Carissimi, who cultivated modal and contrapuntal writing to a higher degree. The harmonic schemes, often emanating out of cadential progression patterns, also result in an unusually regular and symmetrical organization of phrases—a style that would prove to be heavily influential in the second half of the century. These techniques are further supported by an organization of the musical flow with transpositions and sequences, which on the whole gives the impression of a carefully planned structure. It is combined with a smoothly flowing melodic style, clearly influenced by the aria style, also in imitative passages. At the same time, however, Graziani's well-balanced melodic phrases reflect the strong Roman Palestrina tradition.

All these components of Graziani's style seem to aim for a high degree of comprehensibility and accessibility, which offers, in turn, an important explanation for the popularity of his music. This tendency can arguably be related to the doctrines and pedagogical traditions within the Jesuit cultural circle in which Graziani was active; rather than exclusivity, the aim was a direct and immediate address.

Performance

The basso continuo part at the start of each of these works is designated "Organum" ("Organo" on the title page of the partbook), and an organ with relatively loud stops should be at the core of the ensemble. At certain points, at least in ensemble sections, the organ might well double the vocal parts, as well as simply providing a harmonic foundation. There are no records of additional instruments such as theorbo, harp, or violone being used for the performances, but such a practice should of course not be ruled out entirely.

Graziani's compositions were written for, and performed by, male singers, with falsettos or castratos taking the upper parts. Performed with one singer to the part in such a large basilica as Il Gesù, the vocal parts must have been executed with a strong and most likely rather shrill and penetrating vocal timbre—the result of a vocal technique based on high-larynx singing and chest breathing. The incorporation of *ripieno* singers in the ensemble sections of certain motets should also not be ruled out.

Graziani's opus 1 is a compilation of liturgical music, originally composed for a specific practical use. Still, it was likely intended both as a homogenous and flexible collection of music, attractive for many potential buyers and users. It is clear from the church records that instrumentalists such as violinists and cornetto players were engaged at the services, and it cannot be ruled out that instrumental sinfonias or concertato parts were at times added to motets such as these. The modern performer too should feel free to adopt a flexible approach to these works; rather than being works of art to be venerated, they represent a repertory to be used in practice.

Notes

1. Stephen R. Miller, "Music for the Mass in Seventeenth-Century Rome: *Messe piene*, the Palestrina Tradition, and the *Stile antico*" (Ph.D. diss., University of Chicago, 1998), 471–72.

2. Rome, Archivum Romanum Societatis Iesu (hereafter ARSI), Rom. 155/II, fol. 343r.

3. Susanne Shigihara, "Bonifazio Graziani (1604/05–1664): Biographie, Werkverzeichnis und Untersuchungen zu den Solomotetten" (Ph.D. diss., Rheinischen Friedrich-Wilhelms-Universität, Bonn, 1984), 59–61 and 65.

4. Based on the list of works and sources in Shigihara, "Graziani," 69–264. It should be noted that Graziani's first two collections of motets for multiple voices do not have opus numbers on the original prints (see plate 1 for the present case), and it is only with his first collection of solo motets from 1652 that "opera terza" appears on the title page. However, in the posthumous *Mottetti a due, tre, quatro, e cinque voci*, opus 20 (1672), an *indice* lists all of Graziani's publications up until that time, and the first is listed as "Mottetti à 2. 3. 4. 5. e 6. voci, Libri cinque, Opera Prima" (with "Libri à 2. 3. 4. 5." referring to the five partbooks). "Opus 1" has continued to be assumed in references to his collection of 1650, as seen, e.g., in *The New Grove Dictionary of Music and Musicians,* 2nd ed., s.v. "Gratiani, Bonifatio," by Stephen Miller.

5. See Alessandro Zocchari, ed., *La storia dei giubilei, volume terzo (1600–1775)* (Rome: Giunti Editore, 1999).

6. Based on documents in ARSI, Chiesa del Giesù 2009, 2009a, and 2011.

7. One exception is a piece of processional music preserved in the archive of Cappella Giulia at St. Peters: a concerto for two choirs in eight parts, *Quam dilecta tabernacula*, in Rome, Biblioteca Apostolica Vaticana (hereafter BAV), Fondo Cappella Giulia XIII-21. It is a comparatively simple and straightforward work in C major, where the overall effect seems more important than refinement of detail.

8. Mark S. Weil, "The Devotion of the Forty Hours and Roman Baroque Illusions," *Journal of the Warburg and Courtauld Institutes* 37 (1974): 218–48.

9. BAV, Segr. Stato, Avvisi 101; Giovanni Simone Ruggieri, *Diario dell'anno santissimo giubileo MDCL* (Rome, 1651), 49–51. A contemporary description was published in *Apparato delle solenne quarant'hore Celebrate nel GIESÙ di Roma l'Anno Giubileo 1650* (Rome, 1650).

10. Ruggieri, *Diario dell'anno santissimo*, 51.

11. Howard E. Smither, *A History of the Oratorio*, vol. 1, *The Oratorio in the Baroque Era: Italy, Vienna, Paris* (Chapel Hill: University of North Carolina Press, 1977), 207–15.

12. Domenico Alaleona, *Storia dell'oratorio musicale in Italia* (Milan: Fratelli Bocca, 1945), 341; Smither, *A History of the Oratorio*, 255–56.

13. Museo internazionale e biblioteca della musica di Bologna, Ms. Q.43. Facs. ed. in *The Italian Oratorio 1650–1800: Works in a Central Baroque and Classic Tradition*, ed. Joyce L. Johnson and Howard E. Smither, vol. 1 (New York: Garland, 1986).

14. "Adi 15 Giugno morse a Marino in tre giorni il Signor Bonifacio Gratiani quale lasciò le opere grosse et ecclesiatiche a questa Chiesa"; ARSI, Chiesa del Giesù 2011.

15. ARSI, Rom. 240, fols. 94r–98v: "Avvisi per il M. di Capella del Sem. Rom." [1622]. See also Raffaele Casimiri, " 'Disciplina musicae' e 'mastri di capella' dopo il Concilio di Trento nei maggiori Istituti Ecclesiastici di Roma; Seminario Romano, Collegio Germanico, Collegio Inglese (sec. XVI–XVII)," part 1, *Note d'archivio* 12 (1935): 1–26.

16. ARSI, Rom. 143/II, fol. 514r and following; Biblioteca della Pontificia Università Gregoriana, Rome: Girolamo Nappi, *Annali del Seminario Romano* [1640].

17. Lars Berglund, "The Roman Connection: The Dissemination and Reception of Roman Music in the North," in *The Dissemination of Music in Seventeenth-Century Europe: Celebrating the Düben Collection, Proceedings from the International Conference at Uppsala University 2006*, ed. Erik Kjellberg, *Varia Musicologica*, vol. 18 (Bern: Peter Lang, 2010), 193–218.

18. Mary Frandsen, *Crossing Confessional Boundaries: The Patronage of Italian Sacred Music in Seventeenth-Century Dresden* (Oxford and New York: Oxford University Press, 2006), esp. 172–244.

Texts and Translations

Edited and Translated by Peter Sjökvist

For the presentation of the texts of the songs in this edition, the following principles have been used. Spelling has generally been retained, with the exceptions of *i* and *j* and *u* and *v*, which have been normalized according to common modern orthography. When different spellings have been used in the original print, the most common variant has been selected for this edition. All types of accents have been deleted. Abbreviations and contractions have been expanded without remark. In the printed text *et* is written with an ampersand (&), which has been altered to *et*. The ligatures æ and œ are written as *ae* and *oe*. Punctuation has been altered to conform to modern standards, as Renaissance practice in this field is often confusing to modern readers. In printed texts the typesetter may often have been responsible for quite a few of the peculiarities. Capital letters have been retained, except for the letters following the initials in the original print, and except when changes in punctuation have been made. In accordance with the practice in Renaissance prints, capital letters are normally used in order to lend extra emphasis to the word in question and are therefore of interest to us.

1. *Hic est panis*

Hic est panis qui de caelo descendit. Hic est panis Angelorum, factus cibus viatorum.

Venite gentes, adorantes eum et dicite: O quam suavis est, Domine, spiritus tuus! O vere nimiam caritatem tuam, dulcissime JESU!

Benedicite Dominum, omnes Angeli ejus, et qui timetis eum, properate, accedite et confitemini, quia non est amor sicut amor JESU.

Alleluia.

This is the bread that came down from heaven. This is the bread of angels, food made for the wayfarers.

Come, people, worship him and say: Oh, how sweet is your spirit, Lord! Oh, the truly great love of yours, sweetest Jesus!

Praise the Lord, all his angels, and you who fear him, hasten, come near and praise him, since no love is like the love of Jesus.

Hallelujah.

2. *Ludite, canite*

Ludite, canite, filiae Sion, in celebratione altissimae Mariae.

Haec Maria caelum aperit, infernum operit et super sidera terrena collocat. Luctus et fremitus, lacrimae, gemitus, confundunt inferos.

Haec Maria solvit vincula et reddit praemia. Hostes conterit et penas removet. Jubili moduli, citharae, cantica, sidera replent.

Alleluia.

Play, sing, daughters of Zion, in celebration of Mary the most elevated.

This Mary opens the heaven, closes the underworld, and gives earthly matters a place above the stars. Sorrow and wailing, tears, laments, confound the dwellers of the underworld.

This Mary looses bonds and gives rewards. She destroys enemies and takes away punishments. Joyous chants, harps, and songs permeate the stars.

Hallelujah.

3. *Omnes gentes*

Omnes gentes plaudite manibus, jubilate Deo in voce exultationis.

Quoniam Dominus excelsus gloria et honore coronavit Beatum N. [*name*], virtute praeditum, manibus innocentem, et mundo corde, qui confisus est in eo.

Clap your hands, all people, shout unto God with the voice of triumph.

For the Lord most elevated crowned the blessed [*name*] with glory and honor, gifted with virtue, guiltless in his hands, and with a pure heart, which confided

Praedicavit praeceptum illius, et constitutus est in monte sancto suo. Accepit enim benedictionem a Domino, et misericordiam a Deo salutari suo.

4. Amen dico vobis

Amen dico vobis, petite et accipietis, quaerite et invenietis, pulsate et aperietur vobis.

Omnis enim qui petit accipit, et qui quaerit invenit, et pulsanti aperietur.

Alleluia.

5. Domine, ne in furore tuo

Domine, ne in furore tuo arguas me, neque in ira tua corripias me.

A voce gemitus mei adhesit os meum carni meae.

Laboravi in gemitu meo. Lavabo per singulas noctes lectum meum. Lacrymis meis stratum meum rigabo.

6. Ad mensam dulcissimi

Ad mensam dulcissimi convivii tui, pie Domine JESU Christe, ego peccator de propriis meritis nihil praesumens, sed in tua confidens misericordia, accedere contremisco. Corpus enim et cor habeo multis criminibus maculatum.

O pia deitas, o tremenda majestas, ego miser, inter angustias depraehensus, ad te fontem misericordiae recurro.

Parce ergo mihi, Domine, quis es Salvator meus, et miserere peccatrici animae meae. Solve vincula ejus. Sana vulnera.

O pretiosum et admirandum convivium salutiferum et omni suavitate repletum! Nullum enim convivium est isto salubrius, in quo non carnes vitulorum, sed nobis Christus sumendus proponitur verus Deus.

Panis angelicus fit panis hominum. O res mirabilis: manducat Dominum pauper servus et humilis.

Accedite ergo omnes ad manducandum illud. Properate, festinate, currite. Quia dulce et suave est, super mel et favum.

7. Haec est vera fraternitas

Haec est vera fraternitas, quae nunquam potuit violari certamine.

Qui effuso sanguine secuti sunt Dominum, contemnentes aulam regiam, pervenerunt ad regna caelestia.

8. O Jesu, fili Mariae

O JESU, fili Mariae Virginis, miserae spes unica vitae.

JESU, largitor veniae, honor caelestis patriae. Rex virtutum, rex gloriae, rex insignis victoriae.

O JESU, aeterna dulcedo te amantium. Jubilus excedens omne gaudium.

O JESU, veritatis speculum, unitatis signum et charitatis vinculum.

Dum te contemplor in Sacramento, unde me solari tento, inde paenam augeo.

Nam videre te non plene. Quanti luctus, quantae paenae prae dolore morior.

in him. He preached his commands and was established on his holy mountain. For he received a blessing from the Lord and mercy from God his savior.

Verily I say to you, ask and you shall receive, seek and you shall find, knock and it shall be opened unto you.

For everyone who asks receives, and who seeks finds, and unto the one who knocks it shall be opened.

Hallelujah.

O Lord, rebuke me not in your anger, nor chasten me in your wrath.

By reason of the voice of my groaning, my bones cleave to my skin.

I am weary with my groaning. Every night I shall wash my bed. I shall water my couch with my tears.

The table of your sweetest banquet, pious Lord Jesus Christ, I, sinner, daring nothing by my own merits, but confident of your mercy, fear to approach. For my body and my heart are stained by many sins.

O holy godhead, O tremendous majesty, I, wretched, caught in distress, take recourse to you, source of mercy.

So spare me, Lord, who are my savior, and have mercy on my sinful soul. Unbind its chains. Heal its wounds.

O precious and wonderful banquet, salvation-bringing and full of all sweetness! For no banquet is more wholesome than this, in which is offered not the meat of calves, but Christ, true God, to be consumed by us.

Angelic bread becomes bread for men. Oh, what wonder: the lowly and humble servant banquets on his Lord.

Come therefore everyone to this banquet. Hurry, be speedy and quick! For it is sweet and pleasant, more than honey and honeycomb.

This is the true brotherhood, which could never be injured by rivalry.

Those who have shed their blood and followed the Lord, in contempt of royal courts, have reached the heavenly kingdom.

O Jesus, son of Virgin Mary, the only hope of a miserable life.

Jesus, bestower of mercy, honor of the heavenly fatherland. King of virtues, king of glory, king of the remarkable victory.

O Jesus, eternal sweetness for those who love you. Joy surpassing all gladness.

O Jesus, mirror of truth, sign of unity and bond of charity.

When I behold you in the sacrament, whereby I try to comfort myself, I increase the pain thereby.

For to see you not completely. I die from the pain of such great sorrow and such great affliction.

Morior dum cesso mori, tacta spe subliminori vitae, de qua glorior.

9. *Aperi mihi*

Aperi mihi, soror, mea sponsa.
Quia caput meum plenum est rore, et cincinni mei pleni sunt guttis noctium.

10. *Salve, o dulce amoris*

Salve, o dulce amoris convivium.
Anima mea liquescit prae desiderio panis tui.
Cor meum deficit prae dulcedine potus tui.
Quis mihi det pennas columbe, et volabo nec requiescam, nisi in altari tuo, o dulcissime mi JESU.

Hic te gustabo, hic te laudabo, hic vivam, hic moriar, donec inebrier ab ubertate domus tuae, donec satier cum apparuerit gloria tua.

11. *Veni electa mea*

Veni electa mea, et ponam in te thronum meum, quia concupivit rex speciem tuam. Specie tua et pulchritudine tua intende, prospere, procede et regna.

12. *Surge, veni*

Surge, veni, gaude, jubila.
Surge, veni, ascende, N. [*name*]
Pugnasti, vicisti, fidelis fuisti.
Per aquas per ignes invictus transisti ad coronas triumphales, ad torrentes voluptatum, ad beatas caeli sedes, ad aeterna regni praemia.

Surge, veni, coronaberis. Surge, veni, decoraberis, et collocaberis in loco pascue.
Post tenebras lucem sperasti. Ecce quomodo jam splendet, jam coruscat, jam te vestit, jam coronat. Post imbres et procellas expectasti ver floriferum.

Semper florescet, nunquam arescet, in sempiternum dabit odores.
Surge, veni, jucundare. Regna, gaude, delectare.
Alleluia.

13. *Rex magne caelitum*

Rex magne caelitum, prospice ex alto bellantis militis nobilem victoriam.
Rex potentissime JESU, militem respice bellantem. Ille minas tyrannorum, ille tela barbarorum, ille faces despicit.

Adeste lictores.
Adeste procaces.
Tormenta, dolores,
ostendite faces.

Non timet amantis
cor nobile minas,
qui Christi regnantis
amplectitur spinas.

I die when I cease from dying, having tasted the hope of a more elevated life, by which I pride myself.

Open to me, my sister, my bride.
For my head is filled with dew, and my locks with the drops of the night.

Hail, O sweet banquet of love.
My soul melts from desire of your bread.
My heart weakens from the sweetness of your drinking.
Who may give me the wings of a dove, and I shall fly away and not repose, unless on your altar, O my sweetest Jesus.

Here I shall taste you, here I shall praise you, here I shall live, here I shall die, until I am saturated from the richness of your house, until I am satisfied when your glory appears.

Come my chosen one, and I shall place my throne in you, since the king has desired your beauty. With your comeliness and your beauty set out, proceed prosperously and reign.

Rise, come, be glad, rejoice.
Rise, come, ascend, [*name*].
You fought, you won, you were faithful.
You went unconquered through water and fire to the crowns of triumph, to the streams of pleasure, to the blessed abodes of heaven, to the rewards of the eternal kingdom.
Rise, come, you shall be crowned. Rise, come, you shall be decorated, and you shall dwell in green pastures.
You hoped for light after the darkness. Behold how it now shines, it now glitters, it now arrays you, it now crowns you. You awaited the flower-bearing spring after storms and thunder.
It shall always bloom, it shall never be dry, it shall emit pleasant odors forever.
Rise, come, rejoice. Reign, be glad, delight.
Hallelujah.

Great king of heaven, from the heights procure a noble victory for the war-waging soldier.
Jesus, most mighty king, protect the war-waging soldier. He despises threats of tyrants, spears of barbarians, and firebrands.

Come hither, hangmen.
Come hither, bold people.
Show the anguish, the pain,
and the firebrands.

The noble heart of a loving person
does not fear threats,
who embraces the thorns
of Christ, the ruler.

Ite martis, ite mortis, turba saeva ministrorum.	March, you savage troop, promoters of war and death.
Tingite rigidas sanguine manus.	Soak your stern hands with blood.
Sunt regia vulnera reges quae pariunt caelo.	They are royal wounds that create kings for heaven.
Apponite flammas.	Set fires.
Supponite faces.	Add torches.
Has cupit amenas	The soul desires
mens vincula paenas.	these sweet punishments as their fetters.
Dent spicula dextre	May the arrows skillfully bring about
tormenta, dolorem.	anguish and pain.
Hac caelo meliorem	The wounds give a life in heaven
dant vulnera vitam.	that is better than this.
Gaude, felix triumphator, florea caelum tibi serta parat.	Rejoice, fortunate triumpher, heaven prepares flowering garlands for you.
Adeste lictores.	Come hither, hangmen.
Adeste frequentes,	Come hither, in great numbers,
et mortis ardores	and drive away the harmful
jactate nocentes.	flames of death.
Aptate flagellis	Add newly discovered
inventa paenarum.	punishments to the whips.
Haec dabunt in caelis	These shall give a crown
coronam stellarum.	of stars in heaven.

14. *Anima nostra*

Anima nostra sicut terra sine aqua tibi. Perfla, Domine, et induc in virtute tua austrum de caelo sancto tuo.

Venite sitientes, venite ad aquas, quoniam Dominus percussit petram, et fluxerunt aquae et torrentes inundaverunt.

Venite sitientes, venite. Haurietis aquas in gaudio de fontibus Salvatoris.

For you our soul is like soil in want of water. Blow, O Lord, and in your virtue bring forward a wind from your holy heaven.

Come, you thirsty, come to the water, since the Lord struck the rock, and water sprang forth and streams overflowed.

Come, you thirsty, come. In happiness you shall drink water from the sources of the savior.

15. *Quid est hoc*

Quid est hoc quod sentio?
Quis est ignis qui calefacit cor meum?
Quae est lux quae irradiat cor meum?
O ignis, qui semper ardes, et nunquam extingueris, accende me!
O lux, quae semper luces, et nunquam obfuscaris, illumina me!
O utinam arderem ex te! Ignis sancte, quam dulciter ardes, quam secrete luces, quam desideranter aduris!

Veh iis, qui non ardent ex te.

What is this that I feel?
What is the fire that warms my heart?
What is the light that illumines my heart?
O fire, you who burn always and are never extinguished, kindle me!
O light, you who shine always and are never darkened, illuminate me!
Oh, I wish I burned from you! Holy fire, how sweetly you burn, how you shine in secret, how eagerly you set fire!

Woe unto them, who do not burn from you.

16. *O principes*

O principes, attollite portas Jerusalem.

Currite, advolate cum sertis et palmis, cum gemmis et floribus, currite, advolate, Beata Virgo prope est.

Ecce venimus, ecce adsumus, sed quid cernimus.

O mirabile spectaculum! Beata Virgo puris undique cincta radiis sole clarior procedit.

Nostris undique cincta civibus pompa venit triumphali, et decore nuptiali spirat auras adorata.

O princes, lift up the gates of Jerusalem.

Hasten, run closer with garlands and palms, with pearls and flowers, hasten, run closer, the blessed Virgin is near.

Lo! we have come, lo! we are here, but what do we see.

O wonderful miracle! The blessed Virgin proceeds brighter than the sun, surrounded by shining rays.

She comes in a procession of triumph, surrounded by our citizens, and she breathes the air, honored with bridal splendor.

Sed videte, sui sponsi nostri Principis fertur brachiis.

In hoc nobili triumpho ipse Deus currus est.
Dulces citharas ergo tangite.
Pulcros flores ergo fundite.
Hymnos dicite, serta spargite, palmas sternite.
Hymnis, canticis, et floribus, sertis, palmis, et coronis, jubilantes, exultantes, congaudentes et laetantes, veneremur Beatam Virginem triumphantem.

17. *Venite gentes*

Venite gentes, properate omnes.
Si quis sitit, ecce fons aque vivae.
Si quis esurit, ecce panis vitae, panis angelorum.

Si quis friget, ecce ignis, qui semper ardet et nunquam extinguitur.
Si quis estuat, ecce sponsus animarum, ubi cubat in meridie juxta rivulos aquarum.
Ecce Deus noster nobiscum est, Deus noster et omnia.

18. *Justus ut palma*

Justus ut palma florebit, sicut cedrus libani multiplicabitur in domo Domini, ad annunciandum mane misericordiam tuam, et veritatem tuam per noctem.

Alleluia.
Beatus vir, qui suffert tentationem, quoniam cum probatus fuerit, accipiet coronam vitae.

But behold, she is carried in the arms of our prince, her bridegroom.

In this noble triumph God himself is the chariot.
Thus move the sweet lyres.
Thus spread out beautiful flowers.
Sing hymns, spread garlands, lay down palms.
We venerate the triumphing blessed Virgin, we rejoice and exult, in joy and gladness, with hymns and songs, with flowers, garlands, palms, and crowns.

Come, O people, hasten all.
If anyone is thirsty, see the source of living water.
If anyone is hungry, see the bread of life, the bread of angels.

If anyone is cold, see the fire that always glows and is never extinguished.
If anyone is warm, see the bridegroom of our souls, where he rests at noon by streams of water.
See our God is with us, our God and our everything.

The righteous shall flourish like the palm tree, he shall grow in the house of the Lord like a cedar in Lebanon, in order to announce your mercy in the mornings, and your truth in the nights.
Hallelujah.
Happy is the man that endures temptation, for when he is tried he shall receive the crown of life.

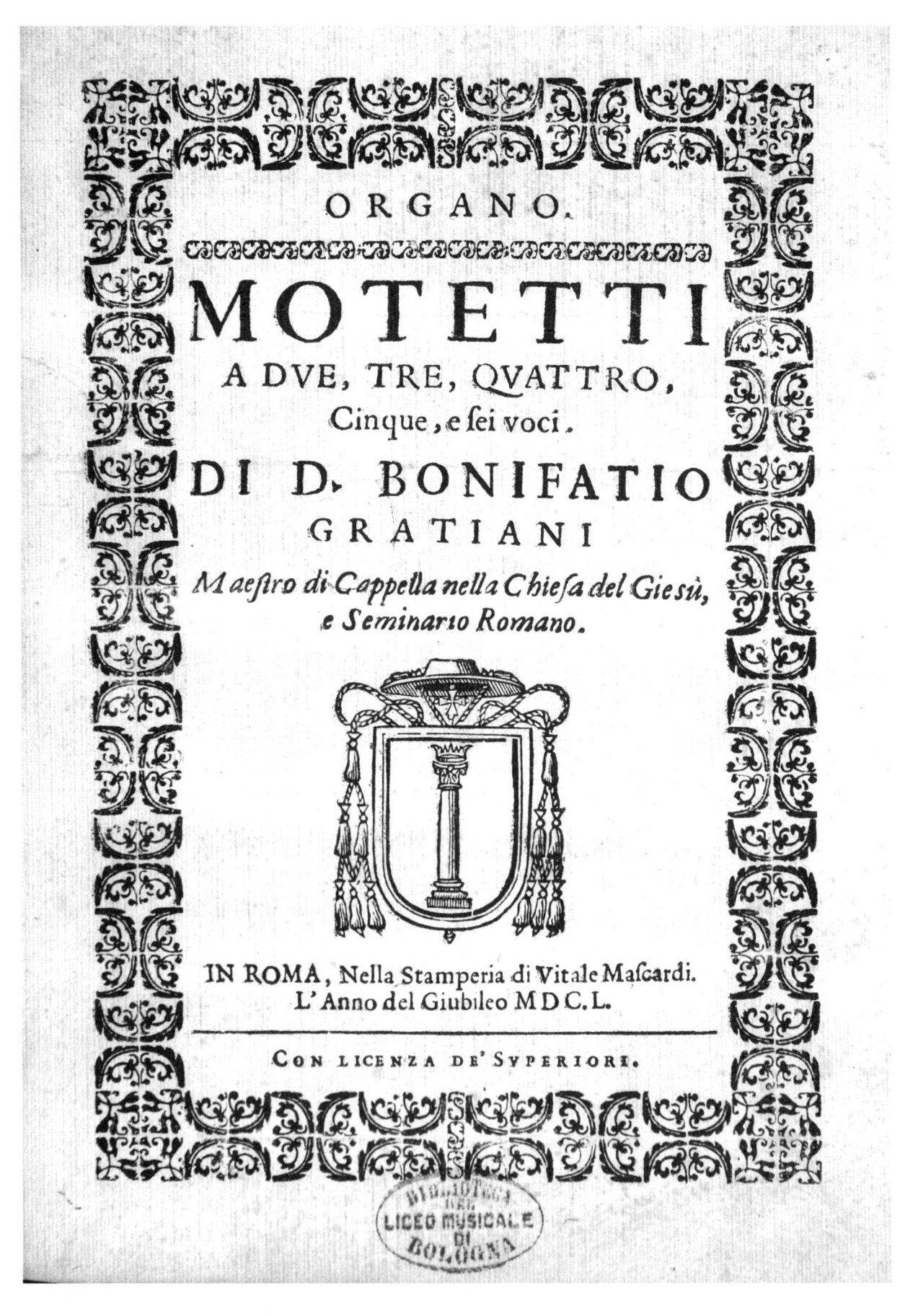

Plate 1. Bonifazio Graziano, *Motetti a due, tre, quattro, cinque, e sei voci* (1650), Organo partbook, title page. Courtesy of the Museo internazionale e biblioteca della musica di Bologna.

Plate 2. Bonifazio Graziano, *Motetti a due, tre, quattro, cinque, e sei voci* (1650), Cantus primus partbook, first page of "Ludite, canite." Courtesy of the Museo internazionale e biblioteca della musica di Bologna.

Motets for Two to Six Voices

Opus 1

Dedication

ALL' EMIN.^(MO) E REV.^(MO) SIG.^(RE)
IL SIGNOR CARDINALE COLONNA.

LA Musica Sirena, famosa Insegna de Colonnesi Heroi, quella che là nel Mar di Corintho, nell'ecclissar dell'Otthomannica Luna, seppe si ben cantar i trionfi, e le glorie de'grandi Avi di V. E. si fa dovuti gl'humili ossequii di tutti i Musici, e molto più di quelli, ch'il cielo se degni di nascerli soggetti e tributarii, tra' quali anch'io mi glorio d'esser per mia fortuna annumerato. Onde per tal ragione non doveano questi miei musicali Componimenti offerirsi ad altri, che à V. E. mio natural Signore in segno dell'humilissimo ossequio, e servitù, che li professo. Spero, che la gloriosa sua COLONNA, quale hò eletta per sicoro sostegno di queste poche debolezze del mio ingegno non men dell'altra, che nell'Egitto fù luminosa scorta al Popolo eletto, sia anco per communicar loro tanto di luce, che rischiarando il fosco de' proprii difetti non habbian da temere le tenebre dell'oblivione: et humilissimamente me l'inchino.

Di Vostra Emininza
Humilissimo, et obligatiss. Servitore
Bonifatio Gratiani.

To His Eminence, the Most Reverent Sir
Sir Cardinal Colonna

The Siren of Music, the famous emblem of the Colonna heroes, who at the Corinthian sea, at the eclipse of the Ottoman moon, knew how to sing of triumphs, and the glories of the great ancestors of Your Eminence, is worthy to be made known thanks to the humble homages of all musicians, and much more by those, who the heaven condescends to let be born as subjects and tributaries [i.e., to the Colonna family], among whom also I myself am proud to be counted, to my own fortune. So that for this reason, these my musical compositions do not have to offer themselves to others than to Your Eminence, my natural Lord, in a sign of most humble homage and servitude, that I profess to you. I hope, that your glorious Column, which I have elected as a safe support for these small weaknesses of my talent, no less than that other [column], which in Egypt made up the illuminated escort to the elected people, is yet to communicate much of their light, illuminating the gloom of their defects, not having to fear the darkness of oblivion: and most humbly I bow.

Your Eminence's
Most humble and obliged servant
Bonifatio Gratiani

1. Hic est panis

28
C1
qui de cae- lo de- scen- dit, ⟨qui de cae- lo de- scen-
C2
cae- lo, qui de cae- lo de- scen- dit,
Org.
4 3 ♯ 4 3
36
C1
-dit,⟩ de cae- - lo de-
C2
de- scen- - - - dit,
Org.
7 6 ♯
41
C1
-scen- - - - dit, de cae-
C2
de cae- - lo de- scen-
Org.
7 6
46
C1
- - lo de- scen- dit, de- scen- dit.
C2
- - dit, de cae- lo de- scen- dit.
Org.
7 ♯ ♯ 4 3

51
C1
Hic est pa- nis An- ge- lo- rum,
C2
fac- tus ci- bus vi- a- to- rum.
Org.
7 6 7 6 ♯
56
C1
Ve- ni- te gen- tes, ⟨ve- ni- te gen- tes,⟩ ve- ni- te,
C2
Ve- ni- te gen- tes, ⟨ve- ni- te gen- tes,⟩ ve- ni- te,
Org.
♯ 6 6 6 6 5 4 3
62
C1
a- do- ran- - tes e- um et di- ci-
C2
a- do- ran- - - tes e- um et di- ci-
Org.
5 6 5 ♯ 6 5 6 4 3
66
C1
-te, a- do- ran- - tes e- - um et di- ci- te, et di- ci- te:
C2
-te, a- do- ran- - tes e- - um et di- ci- te, et di- ci- te:
Org.
6 6 ♯ 4 3

70
C1
C2
Org.
O vere
O quam su- a- vis est, Do- mi- ne, spi- ri- tus tu- us!
75
ni- mi-am ca- ri- ta-tem tu- am, dul-cis- - si- me JE- SU! Be- ne- di- ci- te
Be- ne- di- ci- te
80
Do- mi- num, ⟨be- ne- di- ci- te Do- mi- num,⟩ om- - nes
Do- mi- num, ⟨be- ne- di- ci- te Do- mi- num,⟩ om- - nes
86
An- - ge- li e- jus, et qui ti- me- tis
An- - ge- li e- jus, et qui ti- me- - tis e-

92
C1
e- um, pro- pe- ra- te, ac- ce- di- te et con- fi- te- mi- ni, pro- pe-
C2
- um, pro- pe- ra- te, ac- ce- di- te et con- fi- te- mi- ni, pro- pe-
Org.
95
-ra- te, ac- ce- di- te et con- fi- te- mi- ni, et con- fi- te- mi- ni,
-ra- te, ac- ce- di- te et con- fi- te- mi- ni, et con- fi- te- mi- ni,
98
qui- a non est a- mor sic- ut a- mor JE- SU,
qui- a non est a- mor sic- ut
102
qui- a non est a- mor sic- ut a- mor JE- - SU, ⟨qui- a non est
a- mor JE- SU, qui- a non est a- mor sic- ut a- mor JE-

106
C1
a- mor sic- ut a- mor JE- SU,〉 sic- ut a- mor JE- SU,
C2
-SU, qui- a non est a- mor sic- ut a- mor JE- SU,
Org.
110
C1
non est a- mor sic- ut a- mor, sic- ut a- mor, sic- ut
C2
non est a- mor sic- ut a- mor, non est a- mor sic- ut a- mor,
Org.
113
C1
a- mor, sic- ut a- mor JE- SU, sic- ut a- mor JE- SU.
C2
sic- ut a- mor JE- SU, 〈sic- ut a- mor JE- SU.〉
Org.
117
C1
Al- le- lu- ia, 〈al- le- lu- ia,〉 al-
C2
Org.

9

145
C1
-ia, ⟨al- le- lu- ia,⟩ ⟨al- le- lu- ia,⟩ al- -
C2
-ia, ⟨al- le- lu- ia,⟩ ⟨al- le- lu- ia,⟩ al- -
Org.
6 6 6 6
151
C1
- - - - -
C2
- - - - -
Org.
♯ 6 6
156
C1
- - le- lu- ia, al- - le- lu- ia.
C2
- - le- lu- ia, al- - le- lu- ia.
Org.
♯ 6 5 ♯ 6 5 4 3

2. Ludite, canite

28
C1
Si- on, in ce- le- bra- ti- o- - ne al- tis- si- mae Ma- ri-
C2
in ce- le- bra- ti- o- - - ne al- tis- si- mae Ma- ri-
Org.
4 3
6
5 4 3
35
C1
-ae. ca- - - ni- te, fi- li- ae Si-
C2
-ae. Lu- di- te,
Org.
6
6
5 4 3
42
C1
-on, lu- di- te,
C2
lu- di- te, ca- - - ni- te, fi- li- ae Si-
Org.
6
6
5 4 3
49
C1
lu- di- te, ⟨lu- di- te,⟩ ca- - ni- te, fi- li- ae Si- on,
C2
-on, lu- di- te, ca- - ni- te, fi- li- ae Si- on,
Org.
6
5 4 3

56
C1
in ce- le- bra- ti- o- ne al- tis- si-mae Ma- ri- ae, in ce- le- bra- ti- o- ne,
C2
in ce- le- bra- ti- o- ne al- tis- si-mae Ma- ri- ae, in ce- le- bra- ti-
Org.
63
C1
in ce- le- bra- ti- o- ne al- tis- si- mae, al- tis- si- mae Ma- ri- ae.
C2
-o- ne, in ce- le- bra- ti- o- ne al- tis- si- mae Ma- ri- ae.
Org.
69
C1
Haec Ma- ri- a cae- -
Org.
72
C1
- lum a- pe- rit, in- fer- - num o- pe- rit
Org.
76
C1
et su- per si- de-ra ter- re- na col- - -
Org.

-locat, et super sidera terrena, terrena collocat. Luctus et fremitus, lacrimae, gemitus, confundunt inferos, confundunt inferos.

Ludite, canite, Ludite, canite, filiae Sion,

15

133
C2
nas re- mo- vet. Ju- bi- li mo- du- li, ci- tha- rae, can- ti- ca,
Org.
137
C1
Ju- bi- li mo- du- li, ci- tha- rae, can- ti- ca, si-
C2
ju- bi- li mo- du- li, ci- tha- rae, can- ti- ca, si-
Org.
140
C1
de- ra re- plent, ju- bi- li mo- du- li, ci- tha- rae,
C2
de- ra re- plent, ju- bi- li mo- du- li, ci- tha- rae,
Org.
143
C1
can- ti- ca, si- de- ra re- plent.
C2
can- ti- ca, si- de- ra re- plent. Lu- di- te, ca-
Org.
149
C1
Lu- di- te, ca- ni- te,
C2
ni- te, fi- li- ae Si- on,
Org.

156
C1
fi- li- ae Si- on, in ce- le- bra- ti- o- ne al- tis- si- mae Ma- ri-
C2
in ce- le- bra- ti- o- ne al- tis- si- mae, al- tis- si- mae Ma- ri-
Org.
163
-ae, in ce- le- bra- ti- o- ne, ⟨in ce- le- bra- ti- o- ne⟩ al- tis- si- mae, al- tis- si- mae
-ae, in ce- le- bra- ti- o- ne, ⟨in ce- le- bra- ti- o- ne⟩ al- tis- si- mae
170
Ma- ri- ae. Al- le- lu- ia, al- - -
Ma- ri- ae.
175
- - le- lu- ia,
Al- le- lu- ia, al- -

179
C1
al- le- lu- ia, al- -
C2
- le- lu- ia, al- le- lu- ia, al-
Org.
182
C1
- le- lu- ia, ⟨al- le- lu- ia,⟩ al-
C2
- - le- lu- ia,
Org.
186
C1
- - le- lu- ia,
C2
al- le- lu- ia, al- -
Org.
190
C1
al- le- lu- ia, al-
C2
- - - le- lu- ia, ⟨al- le- lu- ia,⟩ al-
Org.

194
C1
- - le- lu- ia, ⟨al- le- lu- ia,⟩ al-
C2
- - le- lu- ia, al- le- lu- ia, al-
Org.
198
C1
- - le- lu- ia, ⟨al- le- lu- ia,⟩ al-
C2
- - le - lu- - ia, al- le- lu- ia, al-
Org.
202
C1
- - -
C2
- - -
Org.
205
C1
- - le- lu- ia, ⟨al- - le- lu- ia.⟩
C2
- - le- lu- ia, al- - le- lu- ia.
Org.

3. Omnes gentes

25
C1
- - di- te, plau- di- te ma- ni- bus,
C2
- - di- te, plau- di- te ma- ni- bus,
Org.
30
C1
ju- bi- la- te De- o, ⟨ju- bi- la- te De- o⟩ in vo- ce ex- ul- ta- ti- o-
C2
ju- bi- la- te De- o, ⟨ju- bi- la- te De- o⟩ in vo- ce ex- ul-
Org.
33
C1
-nis, in vo- ce ex- ul- ta- ti- o- - nis.
C2
-ta- ti- o- nis, in vo- ce ex- ul- ta- ti- o- - nis.
Org.
37
C1
Quo- ni- am Do- mi- nus ex- cel- sus glo- - - ri- a et ho-
C2
Org.

44
C1
-no- re co- ro- na- - - - vit Be- a- tum
C2
Org.
51
C1
N.,
C2
Quo- ni- am Do- mi- nus ex- cel- sus glo- - - ri- a
Org.
58
C1
C2
et ho- no- re co- ro- na- - - - vit Be-
Org.
65
C1
quo- ni- am Do- mi- nus ex- cel- sus glo-
C2
-a- tum N., quo- ni- am Do- mi- nus ex- cel- sus glo-
Org.

72
C1
- - ri- a et ho- no- re co- ro- na- -
C2
- - ri- a et ho- no- re co- ro- na- -
Org.
79
C1
- - vit, co- ro- na- - - - vit Be- a-
C2
- - vit, co- ro- na- - - - vit Be- a-
Org.
86
C1
-tum N., co- ro- na- vit Be- a- tum N.,
C2
-tum N., co- ro- na- vit Be- a- tum N.,
Org.
92
C1
vir- tu- te prae- di-tum, ma- ni-bus in- no- cen- tem, et mun-do cor- de, qui con- fi- sus est in e- o. Prae- di-
C2
vir- tu- te prae- di-tum, ma- ni-bus in- no- cen- tem, et mun-do cor- de, qui con- fi- sus est in e- o. Prae- di-
Org.

97
C1
-ca- vit prae- cep- tum il- li- us, et con- sti- tu- tus est in mon- te sanc- to su- o,
C2
-ca- vit prae- cep- tum il- li- us, et con- sti- tu- tus est in mon- te sanc- to
Org.
102
C1
et con- sti- tu- tus est in mon- te sanc- to su- o, in mon- te sanc- to su- o. Ac- ce- pit e- nim
C2
su- o, et con- sti- tu- tus est in mon- te sanc- to su- o.
Org.
107
C1
be- ne- dic- ti- o- nem a Do- mi- no, et mi- se- ri- cor- di- am a De- o, a
C2
et mi- se- ri- cor- di- am a De- o,
Org.
112
C1
De- o sa- lu- ta- ri, a De- o sa- lu- ta- ri su- o, a De- o sa- lu- ta- ri
C2
a De- o sa- lu- ta- ri, a De- o sa- lu- ta- ri
Org.

117
C1
su- o, et mi- se- ri- cor-
C2
su- o, ac- ce- pit e- nim be- ne- dic- ti- o- nem a Do- mi- no, et mi- se- ri-
Org.
4 3 6 6 9 8
122
C1
- di- am a De- - o, a
C2
-cor- di- am a De- o, a De- o sa- lu- ta- ri, a De- o sa- lu- ta- ri su- o,
Org.
7 6 4 3 ♯ 4 3
127
C1
De- o sa- lu- ta- ri, a De- o sa- lu- ta- ri su- o, a De- o sa- lu- ta- ri su-
C2
a De- o sa- lu- ta- ri, a De- o sa- lu- ta- ri su-
Org.
♯5 6 ♯ 5 4 3 6 ♯ 5 4 3
132
C1
-o, sa- lu- ta- - ri su- o.
C2
-o, sa- lu- ta- - ri su- o.
Org.
♯ 3 4 4 3

4. Amen dico vobis

22
C1
- - tis, quae- ri- te et in- ve- ni- e-
B
quae- ri- te et in- ve- ni- e- - -
Org.
28
C1
- tis, pul- sa- te et a-
B
- tis, pul- sa- te et a- pe- ri- e- tur vo- bis,
Org.
33
C1
-pe- ri- e- tur vo- bis, pul- sa- - te et a- pe- ri- e- tur vo- bis.
B
pul- sa- - te et a- pe- ri- e- tur vo- bis.
Org.
38
C1
Om- nis e- nim qui pe- tit ac- ci- pit, et qui quae- rit in- ve-
B
Om- nis e- nim qui pe- tit ac- ci- pit, et qui quae- rit in- ve-
Org.

45
C1
-nit, et pul- san- ti, et pul- san- ti a- pe- ri- e-
B
-nit, et pul- san- ti, et pul- san- ti a- pe- ri- e-
Org.
49
C1
-tur, et pul- san- - ti, et pul- san- - ti a- pe- ri- e-
B
-tur, et pul- san- ti, et pul- san- - ti a- pe- ri- e-
Org.
53
C1
-tur, ⟨a- pe- ri- e- tur.⟩ Al- le- lu- ia, al-
B
-tur, ⟨a- pe- ri- e- - tur.⟩
Org.
59
C1
- - le- lu- ia,
B
Al- le- lu- ia, al-
Org.

65
C1
B
Org.
⟨al- le- lu- ia, al- - le- lu-
- le- lu- ia, ⟨al- le- lu- ia, al- le- lu-
72
-ia,⟩ al- le- lu- ia,
-ia,⟩ al- le- lu- ia, ⟨al- le- lu- ia,⟩
79
al- - le- lu- ia, al- le- lu- ia, al-
⟨al- le- lu- ia,⟩ al-
86
- - - - - le- lu- ia.
- - - - - le- lu- ia.

5. Domine, ne in furore tuo

13
C1
-ne, Do- mi- ne, ne in fu- ro- re tu-
C2
⟨Do- mi- ne,⟩ ne in fu- ro- re tu- - o ar- gu- as me,
B
-ne, ⟨Do- mi- ne,⟩ ne in fu- ro- re tu- o ar- gu- as me, ar-
Org.
4 3 [3] 2 5 4 3
17
C1
- o ar- gu- as me, ne in fu- ro- re tu- o ar- - gu- as
C2
ne in fu- ro- re tu- o, ⟨ne in fu- ro- re tu- o,⟩
B
- gu- as me, ne in fu- ro- re tu- - o ar- gu- as me, ar- gu- as
Org.
7 6 4 3 2 5 4 3 9 6 5 [4 3]
21
C1
me, ne ar- - gu- as me, ne- que in i- ra tu-
C2
ne ar- gu- as, ne ar- gu- as me, ne- que in i- ra
B
me, ne ar- - gu- as, ne ar- gu- as me, ne- que in i- ra
Org.
[3] 4 3

25
C1
- a cor- ri- pi- as me, ne- que in i- ra tu- a cor- ri- pi- as me.
C2
tu- a cor- ri- pi- as me, ne- que in i- ra tu- a cor- ri- pi- as me.
B
tu- a cor- ri- pi- as me, ne- que in i- ra tu- a cor- ri- pi- as me.
Org.
31
C1
A vo- ce, a vo- ce ge- mi- tus me- i, a vo- ce, a vo- ce ge- - mi- tus me-
C2
A vo- ce ge- - mi- tus me- - i, a vo- ce ge- - mi- tus me-
B
A vo- ce, a vo- ce ge- mi- tus me-
Org.
38
C1
-i ad- he- sit os me- um car- ni me- - ae.
C2
- i ad- he- sit os me- um car- ni me- ae, os me- um car- ni me- ae.
B
-i ad- he- sit os me- um car- ni me- ae, ad- he- sit os me- um car- ni me- ae.
Org.

43
C1
C2
B
Org.
La- va- bo per sin- gu- las noc- tes
lec- tum me- um, la-
La- bo- ra- vi in ge- mi- tu me- o, in ge- mi- tu
50
lec- tum me- um, la- va- bo lec- tum
-va- bo per sin- gu- las noc- tes, per sin- gu- las
me- o, la- bo- ra- vi in ge- mi- tu me- o,
57
me- um, la- va- bo, la- bo- ra- vi in ge- mi- tu me- o, per sin- gu- las
noc- tes, la- bo- ra- vi, per sin- gu- las noc- tes lec- tum
in ge- mi- tu me- o, la- bo- ra- vi in ge- mi- tu me- o,

64
C1
noc- tes, per sin- gu- las noc- tes lec-tum me- um, la-
C2
me- um, la- va- bo per sin- gu- las noc- tes lec-tum me- um, la-
B
per sin- gu- las noc- tes, in ge- mi- tu me- o,
Org.
71
C1
-va- bo, in ge- mi- tu me- o, per
C2
-va- bo, in ge- mi- tu me- o, lec- tum me- um, per
B
per sin- gu- las noc- tes, la- va- bo per sin- gu- las
Org.
78
C1
sin- gu- las noc- tes, la- va- bo. La- cry- mis me- is,
C2
sin- gu- las noc- tes, la- va- bo. La- - cry- mis me- is,
B
noc- tes lec- tum me- um, la- va- bo. stra- tum me- um ri-
Org.

84
C1
C2
B
Org.
⟨la- cry- mis me- is⟩ stra-tum me- um ri- ga-
⟨la- - cry- mis me- is,⟩ ⟨la-
-ga- - bo, la- - cry- mis me-
87
- - bo, la- - cry- mis me-
- cry- mis me- is⟩ stra-tum me- um ri- ga-
-is, ⟨la- - cry- mis me- is⟩ stra- tum
90
-is stra- tum me- um ri- ga- - bo, la- cry- mis
- bo, la- - cry- mis me- is,
me- um ri- ga- - bo, la- cry- mis me- is, la-

93
C1
me- - is stra- tum me- um, ⟨stra- tum me- um,⟩ ⟨stra- tum
C2
la- cry- mis me- is stra- tum me- um, ⟨stra- tum me- um,⟩ ⟨stra- tum
B
- cry- mis me- is stra- tum me- um ri- ga-
Org.
96
C1
me- um⟩ ri- ga- - - bo.
C2
me- um⟩ ri- ga- - - bo.
B
- bo, stra- tum me- um ri- ga- bo. La- bo- ra- vi in
Org.
100
C1
La- va- bo per sin- gu-las noc- tes lec- tum me- um.
C2
La- va- bo per sin- gu- las noc- tes, per sin- gu-las noc- tes lec- tum me- - um.
B
ge- mi- tu me- o. La- va- bo per sin- gu-las noc- tes lec- tum me- um.
Org.

105
C1
C2
B
Org.
La- - cry- mis me- is, ⟨la- - cry- mis me-
La- - cry- mis me- is, la- - cry- mis
stra- tum me- um ri- ga- - - bo,
6 5 9 4 3 4 5 9 8
112
-is⟩ stra- tum me- um ri- ga- - - - bo, la-
me- is, la- - cry- mis me- is stra- tum me- um ri-
la- - cry- mis me- is, ⟨la- - cry- mis me-
4 2 6 7 6 4 ♭3 2 7 6
119
- cry- mis me- is stra- tum me- um ri- ga-
-ga- - - - bo, la-
-is⟩ stra- tum me- um ri- ga- bo, la- - cry- mis
4 ♭3 4 3

125
C1
- bo, la- - cry- mis me- - - is stra- tum
C2
- cry- mis me- is, la- - cry- mis me- is stra- tum
B
me- is, la- - cry- mis me- is stra- tum me- um ri- ga-
Org.
132
C1
me- um ri- ga- - - - -
C2
me- um ri- ga- - - - -
B
- - bo, stra- tum me- um ri-
Org.
138
C1
- bo, stra- tum me- um ri- ga- - - bo,
C2
- bo, stra- tum me- um ri- ga- - bo, stra- tum
B
-ga- - - - bo, stra- tum me- um ri-
Org.

6. Ad mensam dulcissimi

stratum meum rigabo.

meum, ⟨stratum meum,⟩ ⟨stratum meum⟩ rigabo.

-gabo, stratum meum rigabo.

Ad mensam dulcissimi convivii tui, pie Domine JESU Christe, ego peccator de propriis meritis nihil praesumens, sed in tua confidens misericordia, accedere contremisco.

13
C1
Corpus enim et cor habeo multis criminibus maculatum,
Org.
6
17
C1
corpus enim et cor habeo multis criminibus maculatum.
Org.
21
C2
O pia deitas, o tremenda majestas, ego
Org.
25
C2
miser, inter angustias depraehensus, ad te fontem miseri-
Org.
5 6 4 3 4 2
29
C2
-cordiae recurro, ⟨ad te fontem misericordiae recurro.⟩
Org.
34
C1
Parce ergo mihi, Domine, ⟨parce ergo mihi,
C2
Parce ergo mihi, Domine, ⟨parce ergo mihi,
Org.
♯ 6 5 4 3 6 5

38
C1
Do- mi- ne,⟩ quis es Sal- va- tor me- us, et mi- se- re- re pec- ca- tri- ci
C2
Do- mi- ne,⟩ quis es Sal- va- tor me- us, et mi- se- re- re pec- ca- tri- ci
Org.
42
C1
a- ni- mae me- ae. Sa-
C2
a- ni- mae me- ae. Sol- ve vin- cu- la e- jus.
Org.
46
C1
- na vul- ne- ra. Sa- - na vul- ne-
C2
Sol- ve vin- cu- la e- jus.
Org.
50
C1
-ra. Sol- ve vin- cu- la e- jus, sol- ve vin- cu- la e- jus. Sa-
C2
Sol- ve vin- cu- la e- jus, ⟨sol- ve vin- cu- la e- jus.⟩
Org.

-na vulnera, sa- -na vulnera.

Sa- na vulnera, sa- na vulnera.

O pretiosum et admirandum convivium salutiferum et omni suavitate repletum! Nullum enim convivium est isto salubrius, in quo non carnes vitulorum, sed nobis Christus sumendus proponitur verus Deus, sed nobis Christus sumendus proponitur verus Deus.

Panis angelicus, ⟨panis angelicus⟩ fit panis

82
C1
ho- mi-num. O res mi- ra- bi- lis: man- du- cat Do- mi- num
Org.
7
87
C1
pau- per ser- vus et hu- mi- lis. O res mi-
Org.
92
C1
-ra- bi- lis: man- du- cat Do- mi- num pau- per ser- vus
Org.
97
C1
et hu- mi- lis, pau- per ser- vus et hu- mi- lis.
Org.
102
C1
Ac- ce- di- te er- go om- nes ad man- du- can- dum il- lud. Pro- pe- ra- te, fes- ti-
C2
Ac- ce- di- te er- go om- nes ad man- du- can- dum il- - lud.
T
Ac- ce- di- te er- go om- nes ad man- du- can- dum il- lud.
Org.
7 6 4 3

107
C1
-na- te, cur- ri- te, cur- ri- te, cur- ri- te,___ ⟨cur- ri- te,⟩___
C2
Pro- pe- ra- te, fes- ti- na- te, cur- ri- te, ⟨cur- ri- te,⟩ ⟨cur- ri- te,⟩ ⟨cur- ri-
T
Pro- pe- ra- te, fes- ti- na- te, cur- ri- te, cur- ri- te, cur- ri-
Org.
112
C1
___ cur- ri- te. Pro- pe- ra- te, fes- ti- na- te, cur- ri- te, cur- ri-
C2
-te,⟩ ⟨cur- ri- te.⟩ Pro- pe- ra- te, fes- ti- na- te, cur- ri-
T
-te, ⟨cur- ri- te.⟩ Pro- pe- ra- te, fes- ti-
Org.
116
C1
-te, cur- ri- te. Qui- a dul-
C2
-te, cur- ri- te. et su- a- ve est,
T
-na- te, cur- ri- te. Qui- a dul- ce et su-
Org.

122
C1
-ce et su- a- ve est, qui- a dul- ce
C2
qui- a dul- ce, qui- a dul- ce et su-
T
-a- ve est, qui- a dul- ce et su- a- ve est,
Org.
129
C1
et su- a- ve est, su- per mel et fa- -
C2
-a- ve, su- a- ve est, su- per mel et fa-
T
et su- a- ve est, su- per mel et fa-
Org.
135
C1
-vum, su- per mel et fa- vum. Qui- a dul-
C2
-vum, ⟨su- per mel et fa- vum.⟩ et su- a- ve est,
T
-vum, ⟨su- per mel et fa- vum.⟩ Qui- a dul- ce et su-
Org.

142
C1
-ce et su- a- ve est, qui- a dul- ce
C2
qui- a dul- ce, qui- a dul- ce et su-
T
-a- ve est, qui- a dul- ce et su- a- ve
Org.
6 ♭ 4 3
149
C1
et su- a- ve est, su- per mel et fa- -
C2
-a- ve, su- a- ve est, su- per mel et fa-
T
est, et su- a- ve est, su- per mel et fa-
Org.
♭ ♭ 4 3
155
C1
-vum, su- per mel et fa- vum, ⟨su- per mel et fa- vum.⟩
C2
-vum, ⟨su- per mel et fa- vum,⟩ su- per mel, su- per mel et fa- vum.
T
-vum, ⟨su- per mel et fa- vum,⟩ ⟨su- per mel et fa- vum.⟩
Org.
4 3 ♭ 4 3

7. Haec est vera fraternitas

11
C1
- mi- ne, quae nun- quam po- tu- it, ⟨quae nun- quam po- tu- it⟩ vi- o-
C2
- mi- ne, haec est ve- - ra fra- ter-
B
haec est ve- - ra fra- ter- ni- tas,
Org.
14
C1
-la- ri cer- ta- - mi-ne, ve- - ra fra- ter- ni-
C2
- ni- tas, quae nun- quam po- tu- it vi- o- la- ri cer- ta-
B
⟨haec est ve- - ra fra- ter- ni- tas,⟩ quae nun- quam
Org.
17
C1
-tas, quae nun- quam po- tu- it, ⟨quae nun- quam po- tu- it⟩ vi- o- la- ri cer-
C2
- mi- ne, ve- - ra fra- ter- ni- tas, quae nun- quam
B
po- tu- it vi- o- la- ri cer- ta- -
Org.

20
C1
-ta- - mi- ne, nun- quam po- tu-
C2
po- tu- it vi- o- la- - ri cer- ta- mi- ne, cer- ta-
B
- mi- ne, cer- ta- - mi- ne, cer- ta-
Org.
4 3 5 6
23
C1
-it, nun- quam po- tu- it, nun- quam po- tu- it vi- o- la- ri cer- ta- mi- ne.
C2
- mi- ne, nun- quam po- tu- it vi- o- la- ri cer- ta- mi- ne.
B
- mi- ne, nun- quam po- tu- it vi- o- la- ri cer- ta- mi- ne.
Org.
5 6 ♭ 4 3
27
C1
se- cu- ti sunt,
C2
se- cu- ti sunt,
B
Qui ef- fu- - so san- gui- ne se- cu- ti
Org.
♭ ♯

31
C1
⟨se- cu- ti sunt⟩ Do- mi- num, qui ef- fu-
C2
⟨se- cu- ti sunt⟩ Do- mi- num, qui ef- fu- so
B
sunt, ⟨se- cu- ti sunt⟩ Do- mi- num,
Org.
35
-so san- gui- ne se- cu- ti sunt Do- - mi- num,
san- gui- ne se- cu- ti sunt Do- - mi- num,
se- cu- ti sunt, ⟨se- cu- ti sunt⟩ Do- mi- num,
39
con- tem- nen- tes au- lam re- gi- am, con- tem- nen- tes au- lam re- gi- am, per- ve- ne- runt
con- tem- nen- tes au- lam re- gi- am, ⟨con- tem- nen- tes au- lam re- gi- am,⟩ per- ve- ne- runt
con- tem- nen- tes au- lam re- gi- am, ⟨con- tem- nen- tes au- lam re- gi- am,⟩ per- ve- ne- runt

43
C1
C2
B
Org.
ad re- gna, ad re- - - - gna cae-
6 6
49
-le- sti- a,
ad re- gna cae- le- sti-
ad re- gna, ad re- - - gna, ⟨ad re- gna⟩ cae- le- sti-
ad
4 3 4 3
56
-a,
ad re- gna,
-a,
ad
re- gna, ad re- - - gna cae- le- sti- a,
6 6 4 3

62
C1
ad re- - - gna cae- le- sti- a,
C2
re- gna, ad re- - - gna cae- le- sti- a,
B
ad re- - - gna cae- le- sti- a,
Org.
6
4 3
68
C1
con- tem- nen- tes au- lam re- gi- am, per- ve- ne- runt ad
C2
con- tem- nen- tes au- lam re- gi- am, per- ve- ne- runt
B
con- tem- nen- tes au- lam re- gi- am, per- ve- ne- runt ad re- gna,
Org.
6
73
C1
re- gna, ad re- gna cae- le- sti- a,
C2
ad re- gna, ⟨ad re- gna cae- le- sti- a,⟩
B
ad re- gna, ad re-
Org.
4 3

79
C1
ad re- gna, ad re- gna cae- le- sti- a,
C2
ad re- gna cae- le- sti- a,
B
- - gna cae- le- sti- a, ad re- gna cae- le- sti- a,
Org.
4 3 ♯ 4 3
86
C1
con- tem- nen- tes au- lam re- gi- am, per- ve- ne- runt ad re- gna, ad
C2
con- tem- nen- tes au- lam re- gi- am, per- ve- ne- runt
B
con- tem- nen- tes au- lam re- gi- am, per- ve- ne- runt
Org.
♭ ♭ 6 ♯ ♭
91
C1
re- - - - gna, ⟨ad re- gna⟩ cae- le- sti- a,
C2
ad re- gna, ad
B
ad
Org.
♭ 6 ♯ 4 3 ♭

98
C1
ad
C2
re- - - - - gna cae- le- sti-
B
re- gna, ad re- - - - gna cae- le- sti-
Org.
4 3
104
C1
re- gna, ad re- - gna, ad re- - gna cae- le- sti-
C2
-a, ad re- gna, ad re- - gna cae- le- sti-
B
-a, ad re- gna, ad re- - gna cae- le- sti-
Org.
4 3
110
C1
-a, ad re- - - gna cae- le- sti- a.
C2
-a, ad re- - - gna cae- le- sti- a.
B
-a, ad re- - - gna cae- le- sti- a.
Org.
6
4 3

8. O Jesu, fili Mariae

Cantus 1: O JE- SU, fi- li Ma- ri- ae Vir- gi- nis, mi- se- rae spes u- ni- ca vi- tae, spes u- ni- ca vi- tae, mi- se- rae spes u- ni- ca vi- tae, spes u- ni- ca, spes u- ni- ca vi- tae.

Cantus 1, 2, 3: JE- SU, lar- gi- tor ve- ni- ae, ho- nor cae- le- stis pa- tri- ae.

Cantus 3: Rex vir-

21
C1
C2
C3
Org.
Rex vir- tu- tum, rex glo-
Rex vir- tu- tum, rex glo- - -
-tu- tum, rex glo- - - - ri- ae, rex in-
27
C1
C2
C3
Org.
- - ri- ae, rex glo- ri- ae, rex in-
- - ri- ae, rex glo- ri- ae, rex in- si- gnis vic- to-
-si- gnis vic- to- - ri- ae, rex in- si- gnis vic- to-
6 5 4 3
33
C1
C2
C3
Org.
-si- gnis vic- to- ri- ae, rex in- si- gnis,
- - ri- ae, rex in- si- gnis vic- to- - ri-
- - ri- ae, rex in- si- gnis vic- to- - ri-
4 3
6
5

rex in- si- gnis vic- to- ri- ae.

-ae, rex in- signis vic- to- ri- ae. O JE- SU, ae- ter- na dul- ce- do te a- man- ti-

-ae, in- si- gnis vic- to- ri- ae.

-um. Ju- bi- lus ex- ce- dens om- ne gau- di- um.

O JE-

- SU, ve- ri- ta- tis spe- cu- lum, u- ni- ta- tis si- gnum et cha- ri- ta-

- tis vin- cu- lum, et cha- ri- ta- tis vin- cu- lum.

JE- SU, largitor veniae, honor caelestis patriae.
Rex virtutum, rex gloriae, rex insignis victoriae.

82
C1
-ae, rex in- si- gnis, rex in- si- gnis vic- to- ri- ae.
C2
-ae, rex in- si- gnis vic- to- - ri- ae, rex in- si- gnis vic- to- ri- ae.
C3
-ae, rex in- si- gnis vic- to- - ri- ae, in- si- gnis vic- to- ri- ae.
Org.
90
C1
allegro
Dum te con- tem- plor in Sa- cra- men- to, dum te con- tem- plor in Sa- cra- men- to, un- de me so-
Org.
[allegro]
95
C1
adagio
-la- ri ten- to, in- de pae- nam, in- de pae- nam au- ge- o, un- de me so- la- ri
Org.
adagio
100
C1
ten- to, in- de pae- nam, in- de pae- nam au- - ge- o.
C2
Nam vi- de- re te non ple- ne,
Org.

C2: nam vi-de-re te non ple-ne, vi-de-re te non ple- - ne. Quan-ti luc-tus,

C1: Quan- ti luc- tus,

C1: quan- tae pae- nae prae do- lo- re, do- lo- - re mo- ri-

C2: quan- tae pae- nae prae do- lo- re, do- lo- - re mo- ri-

C1: -or, prae do- lo- re, do- lo- re mo- ri- or. Quan- ti luc- tus,

C2: -or, prae do- lo- re, do- lo- re mo- ri- or. Quan- ti luc- tus,

C1: quan- tae pae- nae prae do- lo- re, do- lo- re mo- ri- or.

C2: quan- tae pae- nae prae do- lo- re, do- lo- re mo- ri- or.

132
C1
Nam vi- de- re te non ple- ne. Quan- ti luc- tus, quan- tae pae- nae prae do- lo- re, prae do-
C2
Nam vi- de- re te non ple- ne. prae do- lo-
Org.
136
C1
-lo- re mo- ri- or, prae do- lo- re mo- ri- or.
C2
-re mo- ri- or, quan- ti luc- tus, quan- tae pae- nae prae do- lo- re, prae do- lo- re mo- ri- or.
Org.
141
C1
Mo- ri- or dum ces- so mo- - ri, mo- ri- or
Org.
145
C1
dum ces- so mo- - ri, tac- ta spe su- bli- mi- no- ri vi- tae, de qua
Org.
149
C1
glo- ri- or, tac- ta spe su- bli- mi- no- ri vi- tae, de qua glo- ri- or.
Org.

JESU, largitor veniae, honor caelestis patriae. Rex virtutum, rex gloriae, rex insignis victoriae.

173
C1
-to- ri- ae, rex in- si- gnis, ⟨rex in- si- gnis⟩ vic-
C2
- ri- ae, rex in- si- gnis vic- to- - ri- ae, rex in- si- gnis vic-
C3
- ri- ae, rex in- si- gnis vic- to- - ri- ae, in- si- gnis vic-
Org.
180
-to- ri- ae, rex vir- tu- tum, rex glo- - ri- ae, rex in- si- gnis,
-to- ri- ae, rex vir- tu- tum, rex glo- - ri- ae, rex in- si- gnis,
-to- ri- ae, rex vir- tu- tum, rex glo- ri- ae, rex glo- ri- ae, rex in-
187
rex in- si- gnis vic- to- ri- ae, rex in- si- gnis vic- to- ri- ae.
rex in- si- gnis vic- to- ri- ae, rex in- si- gnis vic- to- ri- ae.
-si- gnis, in- si- gnis vic- to- ri- ae, rex in- si- gnis vic- to- ri- ae.

9. Aperi mihi

17
A
so- ror, a- pe- ri, ⟨a- pe- ri⟩ mi- hi, so- ror, me- a spon-
T
so- ror, a- pe- ri, a- pe- ri mi- hi, so- ror, me- a spon-
B
so- ror, a- pe- ri, a- pe- ri mi- hi, so- ror, me- a spon-
Org.
24
A
-sa. Qui- - a ca- put me- um ple- num est
T
-sa. Qui- a ca- put me- um, ⟨qui- - a ca- put me- um⟩ ple- num est ro-
B
-sa.
Org.
30
A
ro- re, a- pe- ri mi- hi, so- ror, me- a
T
- re, a- pe- ri mi- hi, so- ror,
B
a- pe- ri mi- hi,
Org.

36
A
T
B
Org.
spon- sa, so- ror, me- a spon- -
me- a spon- sa, ⟨so- ror, me- a spon- -
so- ror, me- a spon- sa, so- ror, me- a spon-
♯ ♭ 4 3
42
-sa.
-sa.⟩ Qui- a ca- put me- um ple- num est ro- -
-sa.
7 6
48
Qui- - a ca- put me- um ple- num est ro- -
- re,
♯ 4 3 ♭ ♭

54
A
- re, qui- - a ca- put me- um
T
qui- - a ca- put me- um
B
Qui- - a ca- put me- um ple- num est ro-
Org.
60
A
ple- num est ro- -
T
ple- num est ro- -
B
- - re, ple- num est
Org.
65
A
- re, et cin- cin- ni me- i
T
- re, et cin- cin- ni me- i ple- ni sunt
B
ro- re, et cin- cin- ni me- i ple- ni sunt gut- tis, ple-
Org.

70
A
ple- ni sunt gut- tis, ple- - ni sunt gut- tis noc- ti- um, ple-
T
gut- tis noc- - ti- um, noc- ti- um, ple- ni sunt gut- tis, et cin-cin-ni me- i
B
- ni sunt gut- tis, et cin- cin- ni me- i, ⟨et cin-cin-ni me- i⟩ ple- ni sunt
Org.
75
A
- ni sunt gut- tis, ⟨ple- ni sunt gut- tis,⟩ ⟨ple- ni sunt gut-
T
ple- ni sunt gut- tis noc- - ti- um, et cin-cin- ni me- i ple- ni sunt gut-
B
gut- tis, ⟨ple- - ni sunt gut- tis⟩ noc- ti- um, et cin-cin- ni me- i,
Org.
80
A
-tis,⟩ ple- ni, ple- ni sunt gut- tis noc- ti- um.
T
-tis, ple- ni, ple- ni sunt gut- tis noc- - ti- um.
B
et cin-cin- ni me- i, ⟨et cin-cin- ni me- i⟩ ple- - ni sunt gut- tis noc- ti- um.
Org.

10. Salve, o dulce amoris

*Come stà**

*See critical note.

-scit prae de- si- de- ri- o pa- nis tu- i, a- ni- ma me- a li-

pa- nis tu- i, a- ni- ma me- a li- que- scit

A- ni- ma me- a li- que- scit prae de- si- de- ri- o pa-

-que- scit prae de- si- de- ri- o pa- nis tu- i, pa- nis tu- i.

prae de- si- de- ri- o pa- nis tu- i, pa- nis tu- i.

-nis tu- i, prae de- si- de- ri- o pa- nis tu- i.

Cor me- um de- fi- cit, cor me- um, cor me- um de- fi- cit,

Cor me- um de- fi- cit, cor me- um, ⟨cor me- um⟩ de- fi- cit, cor me-

Cor me- um de- fi- cit, cor me- um, cor me- um de- fi- cit, cor

26
C
cor me- um, ⟨cor me- um⟩ de- fi- cit prae dul- ce- di- ne po-
A
-um, cor me- um de- - fi- cit prae dul- ce- di- ne
T
me- um, cor me- um de- fi- cit prae dul- ce- di- ne po- tus tu- i,
Org.
30
C
- tus tu- i. Quis mi- hi det pen- nas co-
A
po- tus tu- i. Quis mi- hi det pen- - nas co-
T
po- tus tu- i.
Org.
34
C
-lum- be, quis mi- hi det pen- - nas co- lum- be,
A
-lum- be, quis mi- hi det pen- nas, pen- nas co- lum- be,
T
Quis mi- hi det pen- - nas, ⟨quis mi- hi det pen- nas⟩ co- lum- be,
Org.

38
C
et vo- la- - bo, vo- la-
A
et vo- la- - bo, vo- la- -
T
et vo- la- - bo, et vo- la- bo, vo-
Org.
44
C
- bo, vo- la- bo, vo- - la- bo, vo-
A
- bo, vo- la- - - - bo, vo-
T
-la- - - - - bo,
Org.
50
C
-la- - bo, vo- la- - bo
A
-la- - - - bo, vo- - la- bo
T
vo- la- - - bo, vo- - la- bo
Org.

56
C
nec re- qui- es- - cam, ni- si in al- ta- ri tu- o,
A
nec re- qui- es- cam, ni- si in al- ta- ri tu- - o, o dul-
T
nec re- qui- es- cam, ni- si in al- ta- ri tu- o,
Org.
61
C
o dul- cis- si- me mi JE- SU. Hic te gus- ta- bo, hic mo- ri-
A
-cis- si- me, dul- cis- si- me mi JE- SU. hic vi- vam, hic
T
o dul- cis- si- me mi JE- SU. hic te lau- da- bo, hic
Org.
65
C
-ar, ⟨hic mo- ri- ar,⟩ hic vi- vam, hic mo- ri- ar, hic vi- vam, hic mo- ri-
A
mo- ri- ar, hic te lau- da- bo, hic mo- ri- ar, hic te gus- ta- bo, hic vi- vam, hic mo- ri-
T
mo- ri- ar, hic te gus- ta- bo, hic vi- vam, hic mo- ri- ar, hic vi- vam, hic mo- ri-
Org.

70
C
-ar, hic vi- vam, hic mo- ri- ar, do- nec, do- nec i- ne- bri- er ab u- ber-
A
-ar, hic vi- vam, hic mo- ri- ar, do- nec, do- nec i- ne- bri- er ab u- ber-
T
-ar, ⟨hic vi- vam, hic mo- ri- ar,⟩ do- nec, do- nec i- ne- bri- er ab u- ber-
Org.
76
C
-ta- te do- - mus tu- ae,
A
-ta- te do- - mus tu- ae, do- nec
T
-ta- - te do- mus tu- ae,
Org.
82
C
do- nec sa- ti- er cum ap- pa- ru- e- rit glo- ri- a tu-
A
sa- ti- er cum ap- pa- ru- e- rit glo- ri- a, glo- ri- a tu-
T
do- nec
Org.

88
C
-a, do- nec
A
-a, do- nec sa- ti- er cum ap- pa- ru- e- rit glo- ri- a tu-
T
sa- ti- er cum ap- pa- ru- e- rit glo- ri- a, glo- ri- a tu-
Org.
94
C
sa- ti- er cum ap- pa- ru- e- rit glo- ri- a, glo- ri- a tu-
A
-a, do- nec sa- ti- er cum ap- pa- ru- e- rit glo- ri- a tu-
T
-a, cum ap- pa- ru- e- rit glo- ri- a, glo- ri- a tu-
Org.
100
C
-a, do- nec sa- ti- er
A
-a, glo- - - ri- a tu- a, do- nec sa- ti- er
T
-a, glo- - - ri- a tu- a, cum ap- pa-
Org.

106
C
A
T
Org.
glo- -
cum ap- pa- ru- e- rit glo- ri- a tu- a, glo- -
-ru- e- rit glo- ri- a, glo- ri- a tu- a,
112
- ri- a tu- a, do- nec sa- ti- er cum ap- pa- ru- e- rit
- ri- a tu- a, do- nec sa- ti- er cum ap- pa- ru- e- rit
do- nec sa- ti- er cum ap- pa- ru- e- rit
118
glo- ri- a tu- a, glo- ri- a, glo- ri- a tu- a.
glo- ri- a tu- a, glo- ri- a, ⟨glo- ri- a⟩ tu- a.
glo- ri- a tu- a, glo- ri- a, glo- ri- a tu- a.

11. Veni electa mea

21
C1
ve- ni e- lec- ta me- a, et po- nam in te thro-
C2
ve- ni e- lec- ta me- a,
C3
ve- ni e- lec- ta me- a,
Org.
27
C1
- num me- um,
C2
et po- nam in te thro- - num me- um,
C3
et po- nam in te thro-
Org.
31
C1
et po- nam in te thro- - num me- um,
C2
et po- nam in te thro-
C3
- num me- um,
Org.

35
C1
thro- - num me- um,
C2
- num me- um, thro-
C3
et po-nam in te thro- - num me- um, thro-
Org.
6 7 6 4 3
39
C1
thro- num, thro- num me- um,
C2
- num me- - um, thro- - num me- - um,
C3
- num me- um, thro- - num me- - um,
Org.
4 3 4 3
43
C1
ve- ni, ve- ni e- lec- - - - ta
C2
ve- ni,
C3
Org.
4 3

49
C1
me- a,
C2
ve- ni e- lec- - - - - ta me-
C3
ve- ni,
Org.
55
C1
ve- ni, ve- ni e-
C2
- a,
ve- ni, ve- ni e-
C3
ve- ni e- lec- - - - ta me- - a, e-
Org.
62
C1
-lec- ta me- a, ve- ni, ve- ni, ve- ni, ve- ni,
C2
-lec- ta me- a, ve- ni, ve- ni, ve- ni,
C3
-lec- ta me- a, ve- ni, ve- ni, ⟨ve- ni,⟩ ⟨ve- ni,⟩
Org.

69
C1
qui- - a con- cu- pi- vit rex spe- ci- em tu- am, qui- - a con- cu- pi- vit rex
C2
qui- - a con- cu- pi- vit rex spe- - ci- em tu- am, qui- a con- cu- pi- vit rex
C3
qui- a con- cu- pi- vit rex spe- ci- em tu- am, qui- - a con- cu- pi- vit rex
Org.
77
spe- ci- em tu- am. Spe- - ci- e tu- a, ⟨spe- - ci- e tu- a⟩ et pul- chri- tu- di- ne tu-
spe- ci- em tu- am.
spe- ci- em tu- - am.
85
- a pro- spe- re, pro- ce- de et
in- ten- - de,
in- ten- - de, pro- spe- re, pro- ce-

91
C1
re- gna, ⟨pro- ce- de et re- gna,⟩ spe- ci- e
C2
pro- spe-re, pro- ce- de et re- - gna,
C3
-de et re- gna, pro- spe-re, pro- ce- de et re- gna,
Org.
96
C1
tu- a, ⟨spe- ci- e tu- a⟩ et pul-chri-tu- - di- ne tu- a
C2
in- ten-
C3
Org.
103
C1
pro- spe-re, pro- ce- de et re-
C2
- de, pro- spe-re, pro- ce- de et re-
C3
in- ten- - de, pro- spe-re, pro-
Org.

108
C1
C2
C3
Org.
-gna, ⟨pro- spe-re, pro- ce- de et re- -
- - gna, pro- spe-re, pro-
-ce- de et re- gna, pro- spe-re, pro- ce- de et re-
112
-gna,⟩ pro- spe-re, pro- ce- de et re- gna, et re-
-ce- de et re- - gna,
-gna, ⟨pro- spe-re, pro- ce- de et re- gna,⟩
116
- gna, et
et re- - - gna, et re-
et re- -

120
C1
re- - gna, et re- gna, et re-
C2
-gna, et re- - gna, et re- - gna, et
C3
-gna, et re- gna, et re- gna,
Org.
♯ 4 3 ♯ ♯
124
C1
- gna, et re- gna, et re- gna, et re- -
C2
re- gna, et re- gna, et re- -
C3
et re- - gna, et re- -
Org.
4 2 5 ♯ 4 3
128
C1
-gna, et re- - gna, et re- gna.
C2
-gna, et re- - gna, et re- gna.
C3
-gna, et re- - gna, ⟨et re- gna.⟩
Org.
♯ ♯ 4 3

12. Surge, veni

12
C1
-ni, gau- de, ju- bi- la, gau- de, gau- de, ju- bi- la. Sur- ge, ve- ni, a-
C2
- de, gau- de, gau- de, ju- bi- la, gau- de, gau- de, ju- bi- la. Sur- ge, ve- ni, a-
T
-la, gau- de, gau- de, ju- bi- la, gau- de, gau- de, ju- bi- la. Sur- ge, ve- ni, a-
Org.
♯ 4 3 4 3 ♯
17
C1
-scen- de, a- scen- - de, N. Sur- ge, ve- ni,
C2
-scen- de, a- scen- - de, N. Sur- ge, ve- ni,
T
-scen- - de, N. Sur- ge, ve- ni,
Org.
♯ 6 5 4 3 ♯
23
C1
⟨sur- ge, ve- ni,⟩ a- scen- de, a- scen- - de, N.
C2
⟨sur- ge, ve- ni,⟩ a- scen- de, a- scen- - de, N.
T
⟨sur- ge, ve- ni,⟩ a- scen- - de, N.
Org.
6 5 4 3

30
C1
C2
T
Org.
Pu- gna- sti, ⟨pu- gna- sti,⟩ vi- ci- sti, fi- de- lis fu- i- sti.
Pu- gna- sti, ⟨pu- gna- sti,⟩ vi- ci- sti, fi- de- lis fu- i- sti.
vi- ci- sti, fi- de- lis fu- i- sti.
34
Pu- gna- sti, ⟨pu- gna- sti,⟩ vi- ci- sti, fi- de- lis fu- i- sti.
Pu- gna- sti, vi- ci- sti, fi- de- - lis fu- i- sti.
Pu- gna- sti, vi- ci- sti, fi- de- lis, fi- de- lis fu- i- sti. Pu-
38
Pu- gna- sti, vi- ci- sti, fi- de- lis, fi- de- lis fu- i- sti,
Pu- gna- sti, ⟨pu- gna- sti,⟩ vi- ci- sti, fi- de- lis fu- i- sti, fi-
-gna- sti, pu- gna- sti, vi- ci- sti, fi- de- - lis fu- i- sti,

42
C1
C2
T
Org.
fi- de- lis fu- i- sti. Per a- quas per
-de- - lis fu- i- sti.
fi- de- - lis fu- i- sti.
6
5
4 3
3
47
i- gnes in- vic- tus tran- si- - - sti, tran- si-
Per a- quas per i- gnes in- vic- tus tran-
6 4 3 6 4 3
53
-sti ad co- ro- - - -
-si- - sti ad co- ro- - -
Per a- quas per i- gnes in- vic- tus tran-
6 6

58
C1
- - - nas, per a- quas per i- gnes in-
C2
- - - nas, per i- gnes in-
T
-si- sti ad co- ro- -
Org.
4 3 6 5
63
C1
-vic- tus tran- si- sti ad co- ro- - - nas,
C2
-vic- tus tran- si- sti ad co- ro- - - nas,
T
- nas tri- um- pha- les, per a- quas per i- gnes in- vic- tus tran-
Org.
6 5
4 3 6 6 4 3
68
C1
ad co- ro- - nas tri- um- pha- les,
C2
ad co- ro- - nas tri- um- pha- les,
T
-si- sti ad co- ro- nas tri- um- pha- les,
Org.
♭ 4 3

73
C1
ad tor-ren-tes vo- lu- pta- tum, ⟨ad tor- ren- tes vo- lu- pta- tum,⟩
C2
ad tor-ren-tes vo- lu- pta- tum, ad tor-ren- tes vo- lu-
T
ad tor- ren- tes vo- lu- pta-
4 3
Org.
77
C1
ad tor-ren-tes, ⟨ad tor- ren- tes⟩ vo- lu- pta- tum, ad tor- ren- tes, ad tor- ren-tes vo- lu- pta-
C2
-pta- tum, ⟨ad tor- ren- tes vo- lu- pta- tum,⟩ ad tor-ren- tes vo- lu- pta-
T
- tum, ⟨ad tor- ren- tes vo- lu- pta- tum,⟩ vo- - lu- pta-
4 3 ♯ 4 3
Org.
81
C1
-tum, ad be- a- tas cae- li se- des,
C2
-tum, Sur- ge, ve-
T
-tum, ad ae- ter- na re- gni prae- mi- a.
♯ 4 3 ♯ ♯
Org.

87
C1
C2
T
Org.
Sur- ge, ve- ni, ve-ni, ve- ni, de- co- ra- be- ris,
-ni, ve- ni, ve- ni, co- ro- na- be- ris.
et col- lo-
92
sur- ge, ve- ni, ve- ni, ve- ni, co- ro- na- be-
Sur- ge, ve- ni,
-ca- be- ris in lo- co pas- cu- e, sur- - ge, ve- ni, ve- ni, ve- ni, co- ro- na- be-
96
-ris, et col- lo- ca- be- ris in lo- co pas- cu- e,
et col- lo- ca- be- ris in lo- co pas- cu- e, et col- lo- ca- be- ris
-ris, et

100
C1
et col- lo- ca- be- ris in lo- co
Post
C2
in lo- co, in lo- co pas- cu- e.
Post
T
col- lo- ca- be- ris
in lo- co pas- cu- e.
Post
Org.
104
C1
te- ne- bras lu- cem spe- ra- - - sti.
C2
te- ne- bras lu- cem spe- ra- - - sti.
T
te- ne- bras lu- cem spe- ra- - - sti.
Org.
110
C1
Ec- ce quo- mo- do jam splen- det,
jam co- ro- nat.
C2
jam cor- rus- cat,
jam co- ro- nat.
T
jam te ve- stit,
Post im- bres et pro-
Org.

116
C1
C2
T
Org.
Post im-bres et pro-cel- las ex-pec- ta- sti ver flo- ri- fe- rum.
Post im-bres et pro- cel- las ex- pec- ta- sti ver flo-
-cel- las ex-pec- ta- sti ver flo- ri- fe- rum.
Post
120
ex- pec- ta- sti ver flo- ri- fe- rum, ex- pec- ta- sti ver flo- ri- fe-rum.
-ri- fe- rum. Post im- bres et pro- cel- las ex- pec- ta- sti ver flo- ri- fe- rum.
im- bres et pro- cel- las ex- pec- ta- sti ver flo- ri- fe- rum, ex- pec- ta- sti ver flo- ri- fe-rum.
124
Sem- per, sem- per flo- re- scet,
Sem- per, sem- per flo- re- scet,
nun- quam, nun- quam a- re- scet,

130
C1
in sem-pi- ter-num da- bit o- do- res, in sem-pi-
C2
in sem-pi- ter-num da- - bit o- do- res, da-bit o- do- res,
T
in sem-pi- ter-num da- bit o- do- res, in sem-pi-ter-num da-
Org.
♯ 2 6 7 6 4 3 4 3
135
C1
-ter-num da- bit o- do- res, in sem-pi- ter-num da- bit, da- bit o- do- res.
C2
in sem- pi- ter-num da- - bit o- do- res, in sem- pi- ter-num da- - bit o- do- res.
T
- bit o- do- res, da- bit o- do- res, o- do- res.
Org.
7 6 6 4 5 3 2 6 7 6 4 3 6 4 5 3
140
C1
Sur- ge, ve- ni, ju- cun- da- re. Sur- ge, ve- ni,
C2
Sur- ge, ve- ni, ju- cun- da- re. Sur- ge,
T
Re- gna, gau- de, de- lec- ta- re. Sur- ge, ve- ni,
Org.
7 6 ♯ 4 3 ♯

95

158
C1
C2
T
Org.
piano
forte
- lec- ta- re. Re- gna, gau- de, re- gna, gau- de, de-
- lec- ta- re. Re- gna, gau- de, re- gna, gau- de, de-
de- lec- ta- re. Re- gna, gau- de, re- gna, gau- de, de-
164
piano
[piano]
-lec- ta- re, de- lec- - ta- re. Al- le- lu-
-lec- ta- re, de- lec- - ta- re.
-lec- ta- re, de- lec- - ta- re.
170
-ia, al- le- lu- ia, al- - le- lu- ia,
Al- le- lu-

173
C1
C2
T
Org.
-ia, al- le- lu- ia, al- - le- lu- ia,
Al- le- lu-
7 6 ♯ 4 3 ♯ 7 6
176
al- - le- lu- ia,
al- - le- lu- ia,
-ia, al- le- lu- ia, al-
♯ 4 3 ♯ 4 2
179
piano
al- - le- lu- ia, al- le- lu- ia, ⟨al- le- lu- ia,⟩ ⟨al- le- lu- ia.⟩
al- le- lu- ia, ⟨al- le- lu- ia,⟩ al- le- lu- ia.
- le- lu- ia, ⟨al- le- lu- ia,⟩ ⟨al- le- lu- ia,⟩ ⟨al- le- lu- ia,⟩ ⟨al- le- lu- ia.⟩
7 6 4 3 4 3 [4 3]

13. Rex magne caelitum

C1
-tis- si- me, ⟨rex po- ten- tis- si- me⟩ JE- SU, mi- li- tem
C2
-tis- si- me, ⟨rex po- ten- tis- si- me⟩ JE- SU, mi- li- tem
B
Org.
C1
re- spi- ce bel- lan- tem. Il- le mi- nas ty- ran- no- rum, il- le te- la bar- ba- ro- rum, il- le
C2
re- spi- ce bel- lan- tem. Il- le mi- nas ty- ran- no- rum, il- le te- la bar- ba- ro- rum, il- le
B
Il- le mi- nas ty- ran- no- rum, il- le te- la bar- ba- ro- rum, il- le fa-
Org.
C1
fa- - - ces de- spi- cit.
C2
fa- - - ces de- spi- cit.
B
- ces, il- le fa- - ces de- spi- cit.
Org.

Ad-e-ste lic-to-res. Ad-e-ste pro-ca-ces. Tor-men-ta, do--lo-res, o-sten-di-te fa-ces. Non ti-met a--man-tis cor no-bi-le mi-nas, qui Chri-sti re-gnan-tis am-plec-ti-tur spi-nas, non ti-met a-man-tis cor no-bi-le mi-nas, qui Chri-sti re-gnan-tis am-plec-ti-tur spi-nas, qui Chri-sti re-gnan-tis, qui Chri-sti re-gnan-tis am-plec- - ti-tur spi-nas.

I- te mar- tis, i- te, i- te mor- tis, turba sae- va mi- ni- stro- rum. Tin- gi- te ri- gi- das san- gui- ne ma- nus, tin- gi- te ri- gi- das san- gui- ne ma- nus. Sunt re- gi- a

vul- ne- ra re- ges quae pa- ri- unt cae- lo, sunt re- gi- a (C1, C2, B)

vul- ne- ra re- ges quae pa- ri- unt cae- lo. (C1, C2, B)

Ap- po- ni- te flam- mas. Sup- po- ni- te fa- ces. Has cu- pit a-

-me- nas mens vin- cu- la pae- nas. Dent spi- cu- la

-dextre tormenta, dolorem. Hac caelo meliorem dant vulnera

vitam. Dent spicula dextre tormenta, dolorem. Hac caelo me-

-liorem dant vulnera vitam, hac caelo meliorem, hac caelo me-

-liorem dant vul- - nera vitam.

Gau- de, gau- de, ⟨gau-de,⟩ felix triumphator, gau- de,

Gau- de, ⟨gau- de,⟩ felix triumphator, gau- de,

Gau- de, ⟨gau- de,⟩ ⟨gau-de,⟩ felix triumphator, gau-

126
C1
C2
B
Org.
⟨gau- de,⟩ ⟨gau- - de,⟩ gau- de, fe- lix tri- um- pha- tor, flo-
gau- - de, ⟨gau- de,⟩ fe- lix tri- um- pha- tor, flo-
- de, ⟨gau- de,⟩ ⟨gau- de,⟩ fe- lix tri- um- pha- tor,
4 3
130
- re- a cae- lum ti- bi ser- ta pa- rat, flo-
- re- a cae-lum ti- bi ser- ta pa- rat, flo-
flo- re- a cae-lum ti- bi ser- ta pa- rat,
4 3
134
- re- a, flo- - re- a cae-lum ti- bi ser- ta pa- rat.
- re- a, flo- re- a cae-lum ti- bi ser- ta pa- rat.
flo- - re- a cae-lum ti- bi ser- ta pa- rat.
♯ 6 5 4 3

138
C1
Org.
Ad- e- ste lic- to- res. Ad- e- ste fre- quen- tes, et mor- tis ar-
144
-do- res jac- ta- te no- cen- tes. A- pta- te fla-
150
-gel- lis in- ven- ta pae- na- rum. Haec da- bunt in cae- lis co- ro- nam stel-
156
-la- rum. A- pta- te fla- gel- lis in- ven- ta pae- na- rum. Haec da- bunt in
162
cae- lis co- ro- nam stel- la- rum, haec da- bunt in cae- lis, ⟨haec da- bunt in
168
cae- lis⟩ co- ro- - - nam, co- ro- nam stel- la- rum.

174
C1
Ad- e- ste lic- to- res. Ad- e- ste fre- quen- tes, et mor- tis ar- do- res jac-
C2
Ad- e- ste lic- to- res. Ad- e- ste fre- quen- tes, et mor- tis ar- do- res jac-
B
Ad- e- ste lic- to- res. Ad- e- ste fre- quen- tes, et mor- tis ar- do- res jac-
Org.
181
C1
-ta- te no- cen- tes. Haec da- bunt in
C2
-ta- te no- cen- tes. A- pta- te fla- gel- lis in- ven- ta pae- na- rum.
B
-ta- te no- cen- tes.
Org.
188
C1
cae- lis co- ro- nam stel- la- rum. A- pta- te fla- gel- lis in- ven- ta pae- na- rum. Haec
C2
A- pta- te fla- gel- lis in- ven- ta pae- na- rum. Haec
B
A- pta- te fla- gel- lis in- ven- ta pae- na- rum. Haec
Org.

195
C1
da- bunt in cae- lis co- ro- nam stel- la- rum, haec
C2
da- bunt in cae- lis co- ro- nam stel- la- rum, haec da- bunt in cae- lis, haec
B
da- bunt in cae- lis co- ro- nam stel- la- rum, haec
Org.
201
C1
da- bunt in cae- lis co- ro- - - nam, co- ro- nam stel-
C2
da- bunt in cae- lis co- ro- - - nam, co- ro- nam stel-
B
da- bunt in cae- lis co- ro- - - nam, co- ro- nam stel-
Org.
207
C1
-la- rum, co- ro- - - nam, co- ro- nam stel- la- rum.
C2
-la- rum, co- ro- - - nam, co- ro- nam stel- la- rum.
B
-la- rum, co- ro- - - nam, co- ro- nam stel- la- rum.
Org.

14. Anima nostra

C2
T
B
Org.
C1
per- fla, Do- mi- ne, au- strum de cae- lo sanc- to
per- fla, Do- mi- ne, au- strum de cae- lo sanc- to
per- fla, Do- mi- ne, et in- duc in vir- tu- te tu- a
tu- o, au- strum de cae- lo, ⟨au- strum de cae- lo⟩ sanc- to tu- o.
tu- o, au- strum de cae- lo, au- strum de cae- lo ⟨sanc- to tu- o.⟩
au- strum de cae- lo, ⟨au- strum de cae- lo⟩ sanc- to tu- o.
Ve- ni- te, ve- ni- te si- ti- en- tes, ve- ni- te ad a- quas, ve-
-ni- te, ve- ni- te si- ti- en- tes, ve- ni- te ad a- quas,
quo- ni- am Do- mi- nus per- cus- sit pe- tram, per- cus- sit pe- tram, et flu- xe-

110

67
C1
a- quas, ve- ni- te si- ti- en- tes, ve- ni- te si- ti- en- tes, ve-
C2
a- quas, ve- ni- te si- ti- en- tes, ve- ni- te si- ti- en- tes, ve-
T
ve- ni- te si- ti- en- tes, ve- ni- te, ⟨ve-
B
a- quas, ve- ni- te si- ti- en- tes,
Org.
73
C1
-ni- te ad a- quas, si- ti- en- tes, ve- ni- te ad a- quas,
C2
-ni- te ad a- quas, ve- ni- te, ve- ni- te ad a- quas,
T
-ni- te⟩ ad a- quas, ve- ni- te, ve- ni- te ad a- quas,
B
ve- ni- te si- ti- en- tes, ve- ni- te ad a- quas,
Org.
80
C1
quo- ni- am, ⟨quo- ni- am⟩ Do- mi- nus per- cus- sit pe- tram, per-
C2
quo- ni- am, ⟨quo- ni- am⟩ Do- mi- nus per- cus- sit pe-
T
quo- ni- am, ⟨quo- ni- am⟩ Do- mi- nus per- cus- sit
B
quo- ni- am, ⟨quo- ni- am⟩ Do- mi- nus
Org.

84
C1
-cus- sit pe- tram, per- cus- sit pe- tram, ⟨per- cus- sit pe- tram,⟩ ⟨per-
C2
-tram, ⟨per- cus- sit pe- tram,⟩ ⟨per- cus- sit pe- tram,⟩ ⟨per- cus- sit pe- tram,⟩
T
pe- tram, ⟨per- cus- sit pe- tram,⟩ per- cus- sit pe- tram, ⟨per- cus- sit pe-
B
per- cus- sit pe- tram, ⟨per- cus- sit pe- tram,⟩ ⟨per- cus- sit
Org.
87
C1
-cus- sit pe- tram,⟩ ⟨per- cus- sit pe- tram,⟩ ⟨per- cus- sit pe- tram,⟩ ⟨per- cus- sit pe- tram,⟩
C2
⟨per- cus- sit pe- tram,⟩ ⟨per- cus- sit pe- tram,⟩ ⟨per- cus- sit pe- tram,⟩
T
-tram,⟩ ⟨per- cus- sit pe- tram,⟩ ⟨per- cus- sit pe- tram,⟩ per- cus- sit pe- tram,
B
pe- tram,⟩ ⟨per- cus- sit pe- tram,⟩ ⟨per- cus- sit pe- tram,⟩ per- cus- sit pe- tram,
Org.
91
C1
et flu- xe- - -
C2
et flu- xe- - -
T
et flu- xe- - - runt,
B
et flu-
Org.

98
C1
-runt a- quae, et flu-
C2
-runt a- quae, et flu-
T
et flu- xe- - - runt,
B
-xe- - runt a- quae, et flu- xe- -
Org.
105
C1
-xe- - - - runt a- quae
C2
-xe- - - - runt a- quae
T
⟨et flu- xe- runt⟩ a- quae
B
- runt
Org.
111
C1
et tor-
C2
et tor- ren- tes in- un- da- ve- - runt,
T
et tor-
B
et tor- ren- tes in- un- da- ve- - runt,
Org.

114
C1
-ren- tes in- un- da- ve- - - runt,
C2
et tor- ren- tes in- un- da-
T
-ren- tes in- un- da- ve- - - runt,
B
et tor- ren- tes in- un- da- ve-
Org.
117
et tor- ren- tes in- un- da- ve- -
-ve- - runt, et tor- ren- tes in- un- da-
et tor- ren- tes in- un- da- ve-
- - runt,
120
- - runt. Ve- ni- te si- ti-
-ve- - runt. Ve- ni- te si- ti-
-runt. Ve- ni- te si- ti-
et tor- ren- tes in- un- da- ve- runt. Ve-

124
C1
-en- tes, ve- ni- te, ve- ni- te.
C2
-en- tes, ve- ni- te, ve- ni- te. Hau- ri- e- tis a- quas in gau- di- o de
T
-en- tes, ve- ni- te, ve- ni- te. Hau- ri- e- tis a- quas in
B
-ni- te si- ti- en- tes, ve- ni- te.
Org.
130
C1
Hau- ri- e- tis a- quas in gau- di- o de fon- ti- bus Sal- va- to- ris, in gau- di- o,
C2
fon- ti- bus, in gau- di- o de fon- ti- bus Sal- va- to- ris, in gau- di- o
T
gau- di- o de fon- ti- bus, de fon- ti- bus Sal- va- to- ris, hau- ri- e- tis a- quas,
B
Hau- ri- e- tis a- quas in
Org.
135
C1
hau- ri- e- tis a- quas in gau- di- o de fon- ti- bus Sal- va- to- ris, in
C2
de fon- - ti- bus, de fon- ti- bus Sal- va- to- ris, in
T
hau- ri- e- tis
B
gau- di- o de fon- ti- bus, de fon- ti- bus Sal- va- to- ris,
Org.

139
C1
gau- di- o, in gau- di- o, hau- ri- e- tis a- quas in gau- di-
C2
gau- di- o, hau- ri- e- tis a- quas in gau- di- o de fon- ti- bus,
T
a- quas in gau- di- o de fon- ti- bus Sal- va- to-
B
hau- ri- e- tis a- quas in gau- di- o de fon- ti-
5 6 7 6
Org.
143
C1
-o de fon- ti- bus Sal- va- to- ris, de fon- ti- bus Sal- va- to- ris.
C2
de fon- ti- bus Sal- va- to- ris, de fon- ti- bus Sal- - va- to- ris.
T
-ris, de fon- ti- bus, ⟨de fon- ti- bus⟩ Sal- va- to- ris.
B
-bus, de fon- ti- bus Sal- va- to- ris, de fon- ti- bus Sal- va- to- ris.
4 3 ♭ 6 7 6 3 4 3
Org.

15. Quid est hoc

Quid est hoc, ⟨quid est hoc⟩ quod sen- ti- o? Quid, quid est hoc, ⟨quid est hoc⟩ quod sen- ti- o, hoc quod sen- ti- o?

Quis est i- gnis qui ca- le- fa- cit cor me- um? Quis est i- gnis qui ca-

14
C1
C2
A
B
Org.
Quae est lux quae ir- ra- di- at cor
-le- fa- cit cor me- um?
18
me- um? Quae, quae est lux, ⟨quae est lux⟩ quae ir- ra- - di- at cor
22
O i- gnis, qui sem- per ar- des, et nun- quam ex- tin- gue- ris,
me- um? O i- gnis,
O i- gnis, qui sem- per ar- des, et nun- quam ex- tin- gue- ris,
O

27
C1
C2
A
B
Org.
qui sem-per ar- des, et nun-quam ex- tin- gue- ris, o
qui sem-per ar- des, et nun- quam ex- tin- gue- ris, qui sem-per ar- des,
o i- gnis, ⟨o i- gnis,⟩ qui sem-per
i- gnis, qui sem-per ar- des, et nun- quam, et nun-quam ex- tin- gue- ris, et
6 5 4 3
31
i- gnis, qui sem-per ar- des, et nun- quam, ⟨et
qui sem- per ar- des, et nun- quam ex- tin- gue- ris, qui sem-per ar- des, et
ar- des, et nun- quam, et nun- quam ex- tin- gue- ris, o i- gnis, qui sem- per
nun- quam, ⟨et nun- quam,⟩ o i- gnis, qui sem-per ar- des,
4 3
35
nun- quam,⟩ ⟨et nun- quam,⟩ ⟨et nun- quam⟩ ex- tin- gue- ris,
nun- quam, et nun- quam, ⟨et nun- quam⟩ ex- tin- gue- ris, ac- cen-
ar- des, ac- cen-
qui sem- per ar- des, et nun- quam ex- tin- gue- ris,
4 3 3 3 3 ♭3

accende, accende, accende, accende, accende me! accende, accende de me, accende de me! accende me, accende de me! accende me, accende de me!

O lux, quae semper luces, et nunquam obfus-

53
C1
- ca- ris, il- lu- mi- na me! O lux,
C2
O lux,
A
O lux,
B
Org.
60
C1
quae sem- per lu- ces, ⟨quae sem- per lu- ces,⟩ et nun- quam ob- fus-
C2
quae sem- per lu- ces, ⟨quae sem- per lu- ces,⟩ et nun- quam ob- fus-
A
quae sem- per lu- ces, quae sem- per lu- ces, et nun- quam ob- fus-
B
Org.
66
C1
- ca- ris, il- lu- mi- na me, il- lu- mi- na me!
C2
- ca- ris, il- lu- mi- na me, ⟨il- lu- mi- na me!⟩
A
- ca- ris, il- lu- mi- na me, ⟨il- lu- mi- na me!⟩
B
Org.

72
B
O u- ti-nam ar- de- rem ex te! I- gnis sanc- te, quam dul- ci- ter ar- des, quam se-
Org.
77
B
-cre- te lu- ces, quam de- si- de- ran- - ter a- du- ris!
Org.
81
C1
O u- ti-nam ar- de- rem ex te! I- gnis sanc- - te,
C2
O u- ti-nam ar- de- rem ex te! I- gnis sanc- te,
A
O u- ti-nam ar- de- rem ex te! I- gnis sanc- te,
B
quam dul- ci- ter
Org.
85
C1
quam se- cre- - te lu- ces,
C2
quam se- cre- - te lu- ces, quam de- si- de- ran-
A
quam de- si- de- ran- ter a-
B
ar- des, quam de- si- de-
Org.

89
C1
C2
A
B
Org.
quam de- si- de- ran- ter a- du- ris,
- ter a- du- ris, quam de- si- de-
-du- ris, quam de- si- de- ran- - ter a- du- ris,
-ran- ter, ⟨quam de- si- de- ran- - ter⟩ a- du- ris,
6 4 3
93
quam de- si- de- ran- ter a- du- - ris!
-ran- ter a- du- ris, ⟨quam de- si- de- ran- ter a- du- ris!⟩
quam de- si- de- ran- ter, ⟨quam de- si- de- ran- ter a- du- - ris!⟩
quam de- si- de- ran- ter a- du- - ris!
6 4 3 ♭ 5 6 3 6 4 3
97
Veh i- is, veh, qui non ar- -
Veh i- is, veh, qui non ar- - dent,
Veh i- is, veh i- is, veh, qui non ar-
Veh i- is, veh i- is,
♯

103
C1
- - - - dent ex te, veh i- is,
C2
veh i- is, veh, qui non ar-
A
- - - dent ex te, veh i- is,
B
veh i- is, qui non
Org.
4 3 ♭ ♯
110
C1
veh
C2
- - - - - dent ex te, veh
A
veh i- is, veh,
B
ar- - - - dent ex te, veh
Org.
4 3
116
C1
i- is, qui non ar- - dent, qui non ar- -
C2
i- is, qui non ar- - dent, qui non ar- -
A
qui non ar- - dent, qui non ar-
B
i- is, qui non ar- - dent,
Org.
6 6 ♭ 6

122
C1
-dent, non ar- dent ex te. Veh, veh i- is, qui non ar-
C2
-dent, non ar- dent ex te. Veh, veh i- is, qui non ar-
A
- dent, non ar- dent ex te. Veh, veh i- is,
B
veh, veh i- is,
Org.
130
C1
- - dent, qui non ar- dent ex
C2
- - dent, qui non ar- - - dent ex
A
veh
B
qui non ar- - - - dent ex
Org.
136
C1
te, veh i- is, qui non ar-
C2
te, veh i- is, qui non ar- - -
A
i- is, veh, qui non ar- - - dent ex te.
B
te, veh i- is, qui non
Org.

142
C1
- dent, non ar- dent ex te. Veh i- is, veh i- is, qui non
C2
- dent, non ar- dent ex te. Veh i- is, veh i- is, qui non
A
Veh i- is, veh i- is,
B
ar- dent ex te. Veh i- is, veh i- is, qui non
6 4 3 7 6 ♯
Org.
148
C1
ar- dent, non ar- dent ex te, qui non
C2
ar- dent, non ar- dent ex te, qui non ar- - dent, qui non ar-
A
qui non ar- - -
B
ar- dent, non ar- dent ex te, qui non
6 5 4 3 ♯ ♯
Org.
154
C1
ar- - dent, non ar- dent ex te.
C2
-dent, ⟨qui non ar- dent,⟩ non ar- dent ex te.
A
- dent, non ar- - dent, non ar- dent ex te.
B
ar- - - dent, non ar- dent ex te.
♯ ♯ ♭ 4 3
Org.

16. O principes

12
C1
C2
Org.
at- tol- li- te por- tas Je- ru- sa- lem, at- tol- li- te por- tas, ⟨at-
-tol- li- te por- tas Je- ru- - sa- lem, at- tol- li- te por- tas, ⟨at-
15
-tol- li- te por- tas,⟩ por- - tas Je- ru- sa- lem.
-tol- li- te por- tas,⟩ por- - tas Je- ru- sa- lem.
19
Cur- ri- te, ⟨cur- ri- te,⟩ ad- vo- la- - - -
25
-te, cur- ri- te,
Cur- ri- te, cur- ri- te, ad- vo- la- - - - te,

32
C1
cur- ri- te, ad- vo- la- - te, ad- vo- la-
C2
cur- ri- te, ⟨cur- ri- te,⟩ ad- vo- la- -
Org.
38
presto
C1
- te cum ser- tis et
C2
- te, cum ser- tis et pal- mis, cum gem- mis et flo- ri-
Org.
presto
44
C1
pal- mis, cum gem- mis et flo- ri- bus, cum gem- mis et flo- ri-
C2
-bus, cum ser- tis et pal- mis, cum gem- mis et flo- ri-
Org.
50
C1
-bus, cur- ri- te, ⟨cur- ri- te,⟩ ad- vo- la- te,
C2
-bus, cur- - ri- te, ⟨cur- - ri- te,⟩ ad- vo-
Org.

54
C1
ad- vo- la- te, ⟨ad- vo- la- te,⟩ Be- a- ta Vir- go
C2
-la- te, ad- vo- la- te, Be- a- ta Vir- go pro-
Org.
58
C1
pro- pe est, ad- vo- la- te, ad- vo- la- te,
C2
- pe est, ad- vo- la- te, ad- vo- la- te,
Org.
62
C1
Be- a- ta Vir- go pro- pe est, pro- - pe est.
C2
Be- a- ta Vir- go pro- - pe est, pro- - pe est.
Org.
66
A
Ec- ce ve- ni- mus, ec- ce ad- su- mus, sed, sed quid cer- ni- mus.
T
Ec- ce ve- ni- mus, ec- ce ad- su- mus, sed, sed quid cer- ni- mus.
B
Ec- ce ve- ni- mus, ec- ce ad- su- mus, sed, sed quid cer- ni- mus.
Org.

72
A
T
O mi- ra- bi- le spec- ta- cu- lum! Be- a- ta Vir- go pu- ris un- di- que cinc- ta
Org.
77
A
O mi- ra- bi- le spec- ta- cu- lum!
T
ra- di- is so- le cla- ri- or pro- ce- dit.
Org.
82
A
Be- a- ta Vir- go pu- ris un- di- que cinc- ta ra- di- is so- le cla- ri-
T
Org.
86
A
-or pro- ce- dit. Be- a- ta Vir- go pu- ris
T
Be- a- ta Vir- go pu- ris
B
O mi- ra- bi- le spec- ta- cu- lum! Be- a- ta Vir- go pu- ris
Org.

92
A
un- di- que cinc- ta ra- di- is so- le cla- ri- or, so- le cla- ri- or pro-
T
un- di- que cinc- ta ra- di- is so- le cla- ri- or, so- le cla- ri- or pro-
B
un- di- que cinc- ta ra- di- is so- le cla- ri- or, ⟨so- le cla- ri- or⟩ pro-
Org.
96
A
-ce- dit, so- le cla- ri- or pro- ce- dit.
T
-ce- dit, so- le cla- ri- or pro- ce- dit.
B
-ce- dit, so- le cla- ri- or, ⟨so- le cla- ri- or pro- ce- dit.⟩
Org.
100
C1
No- stris un- di- que cinc- ta ci- vi- bus pom- - pa ve- nit tri- um-
C2
No- stris un- di- que cinc- ta ci- vi- bus pom- - pa ve- nit tri- um-
A
T
B
Org.

104
C1
-pha- li,
C2
-pha- li,
A
et de- co- re nu- pti- a- li spi- rat au- ras a- do-
T
et de- co- re nu- pti- a- li spi- rat au- ras a- do-
B
et de- co- re nu- pti- a- li, ⟨et de- co- re nu- pti- a- li⟩ spi- rat au- ras a- do-
Org.
108
C1
Sed vi- de- te, su- i spon- si no- stri Prin- ci- pis fer-
C2
Sed vi- de- te, su- i spon- si no- stri Prin- ci- pis
A
-ra- ta.
T
-ra- ta.
B
-ra- ta.
Org.

113
C1
- tur bra- chi- is, fer- tur bra- chi- is. O mi-
C2
fer- tur bra- chi- is. O mi-
A
O mi-
T
O mi-
B
O mi-
Org.
♭ 4 3 ♭ 4 3 6
117
C1
-ra- bi- le spec- ta- cu- lum! O mi- ra- bi- le spec- ta- cu- lum!
C2
-ra- bi- le spec- ta- cu- lum! ⟨O mi- ra- bi- le spec- ta- cu- lum!⟩ In hoc
A
-ra- bi- le spec- ta- cu- lum! ⟨O mi- ra- bi- le spec- ta- cu- lum!⟩ In hoc
T
-ra- bi- le spec- ta- cu- lum! ⟨O mi- ra- bi- le spec- ta- cu- lum!⟩ In hoc
B
-ra- bi- le spec- ta- cu- lum! ⟨O mi- ra- bi- le spec- ta- cu- lum!⟩
Org.
4 3 6 4 3 6

135

136

C1: Pul- cros flo- res er- go fun- di- te.

C2: Pul- cros flo- res er- go fun- di- te.

A: er- go tan- gi- te. Hym- nos di- ci- te,

T: er- go tan- gi- te. Hym- nos di- ci- te,

B: er- go tan- gi- te. Hym- nos di- ci- te,

C1: ser- ta spar- gi- te, pal- mas ster- ni- te. Hym- nos di- ci- te,

C2: ser- ta spar- gi- te, pal- mas ster- ni- te. Hym- nos di- ci- te,

A: pal- mas ster- ni- te. Hym- nos di- ci- te,

T: pal- mas ster- ni- te. Hym- nos di- ci- te,

B: Hym- nos di- ci- te,

145
C1
ser- ta spar- gi- te, pal- mas ster- ni- te.
C2
ser- ta spar- gi- te, pal- mas ster- ni- te.
A
ser- ta spar- gi- te, pal- mas ster- ni- te. Hym- nis, can- ti- cis, et
T
ser- ta spar- gi- te, pal- mas ster- ni- te. Hym- nis,
B
ser- ta spar- gi- te, pal- mas ster- ni- te.
Org.
4 3
151
C1
Hym- nis, can- ti-cis, et flo-
C2
Hym- nis, can- ti-cis, et flo- - ri- bus,
A
flo- - ri- bus, ser- tis,
T
can- ti- cis, et flo- - ri- bus,
B
Hym- nis, can- ti- cis, et
Org.
6 7 6

138

161
C1
-ro- nis, ju- bi- lan- tes, ex- ul- tan- -
C2
- nis, ju- bi- lan- tes, ex- ul- tan- -
A
-ro- nis,
T
-ro- nis,
B
-ro- nis,
Org.
4 3 6 6 ♭
166
C1
- tes,
C2
- tes,
A
con- gau- den- tes et lae- tan- -
T
con- gau- den- tes et lae- tan- -
B
con- gau- den- tes et lae- tan- tes, et lae- tan- -
Org.
6

140

141

142

195
C1
-tem, ve- ne- re- mur Be- a- tam Vir- gi- nem tri- um- phan-
C2
-tem,⟩ ve- ne- re- mur Be- a- tam Vir- gi- nem tri- um-
A
-tem,⟩ tri- um- phan-
T
ve- ne- re- mur Be- a- tam Vir- gi- nem tri- um- phan- tem,
B
-tem, tri- um-
Org.

199
C1
- tem, tri- um- phan- tem, ⟨tri- um- phan- tem.⟩
C2
-phan- tem, ⟨tri- um- phan- tem,⟩ ⟨tri- um- phan- tem.⟩
A
-tem, ⟨tri- um- phan- tem,⟩ ⟨tri- um- phan- tem.⟩
T
tri- um- phan- - tem, ⟨tri- um- phan- - tem.⟩
B
-phan- - tem, ⟨tri- um- phan- tem.⟩
Org.

17. Venite gentes

16
C1
Ve- ni- te, ve- ni- te gen- tes, ve- ni- te, ve- ni- te gen- tes,
C2
Ve- ni- te, ⟨ve- ni- te,⟩ ⟨ve- ni- te⟩ gen- tes, ve- ni- te, ve- ni- te gen- tes,
A
Ve- ni- te, ⟨ve- ni- te⟩ gen- tes, ve- ni- te, ve- ni- te gen- tes,
T
Ve- ni- te, ve- ni- te gen- tes, ve- ni- te, ve- ni- te gen- tes,
B
Ve- ni- te, ve- ni- te gen- tes, ve- ni- te, ve- ni- te gen- tes,
Org.
24
C1
C2
pro- pe- ra- te om- nes, om- nes, pro- pe- ra- te,
A
pro- pe- ra- te om- nes, om- nes, pro- pe- ra- te om-
T
pro- pe- ra- te om- nes, pro- pe- ra- te om- nes, pro- pe-
B
pro- pe- ra- te om- nes,
Org.
♮6
♯
4 3

28
C1
pro- pe- ra- te om- nes, om- nes, pro- pe- ra- te, pro- pe- ra- te, ⟨pro- pe- ra- te.⟩
C2
pro- pe- ra- te om- nes, pro- pe- ra- te, pro- pe- ra- te, pro- pe- ra- te.
A
-nes, pro- pe- ra- te, ⟨pro- pe- ra- te,⟩ ⟨pro- pe- ra- te.⟩
T
-ra- te om- nes, pro- pe- ra- te, pro- pe- ra- te, pro- pe- ra- te.
B
om- nes, pro- pe- ra- te om- nes, pro- pe- ra- te, pro- pe- ra- te.
Org.
33
C1
Si quis si- tit,
C2
Si quis si- tit,
A
T
B
ec- ce fons, ec- ce fons a- -
Org.

38
C1
Si quis e- su- rit,
C2
Si quis e- su- rit,
A
ec- - ce pa- nis vi- tae,
T
B
- que vi- vae.
Org.
43
C1
Si quis
C2
Si quis
A
⟨ec- ce pa- nis vi- tae,⟩ pa- nis an- ge- lo- - rum.
T
B
Org.

48
C1
fri- get,
C2
fri- get,
A
T
ec- ce, ec- ce i- gnis, qui sem- per ar- - det et
B
Org.
52
C1
ec- ce spon-sus, ec- ce spon-sus a- ni- ma-
C2
ec- ce spon-sus, ⟨ec- ce spon-sus⟩ a- ni-
A
Si quis e- stu- at,
T
nun-quam ex- tin- gui- tur. Si quis e- stu- at,
B
Si quis e- stu- at,
Org.

57
C1
- rum, u- bi cu- bat in me- ri- di- e ju- xta ri- vu-los a-
C2
-ma- - rum, u- bi cu- bat in me- ri- di- e
Org.
♯ ♯ 6 4 3 7 6
61
C1
-qua- rum, a- qua- rum, ju- xta ri- vu-los a- qua- rum.
C2
ju- xta ri- vu-los a- qua- rum, ju- xta ri- vu-los a- qua- rum.
Org.
7 6 ♯ 6 4 3 6 4 3
65
C1
pro- pe- ra- - - te
C2
pro- pe- ra- - - te
A
Ve- ni- te, ve- ni- te gen- tes,
T
Ve- ni- te, ⟨ve- ni- te⟩ gen- tes,
B
Ve- ni- te, ⟨ve- ni- te⟩ gen- tes,
Org.
6 6 ♯ 6 5

72
C1
om- nes. pro- pe- ra- -
C2
om- nes. pro- pe- ra- -
A
Ve- ni- te, ⟨ve- ni- te⟩ gen- tes,
T
Ve- ni- te, ⟨ve- ni- te⟩ gen- tes,
B
Ve- ni- te, ⟨ve- ni- te⟩ gen- tes,
Org.
79
C1
- te om- nes. Ve-
C2
- te om- nes. Ve-
A
pro- pe- ra- - te om-
T
pro- pe- ra- - - te om-
B
pro- pe- ra- - te om- nes, pro- pe- ra-
Org.

86
C1
-ni- te, ve- ni- te gen- tes, pro- pe- ra-
C2
-ni- te, ve- ni- te gen- tes, pro- pe- ra- - te, pro- pe- ra-
A
-nes. Ve- ni- te gen- tes, pro- pe- ra- - te,
T
-nes. Ve- ni- te gen- tes,
B
-te. Ve- ni- te gen- tes, pro- pe-
Org.
93
C1
- te, ⟨pro- pe- ra- te,⟩ pro- pe- ra- te om- nes. Ec- ce,
C2
- te, pro- pe- ra- - te om- nes. Ec- ce,
A
Ec- ce,
T
pro- pe- ra- - te, Ec- ce,
B
-ra- - te, ⟨pro- pe- ra- - te⟩ om- nes. Ec- ce,
Org.

100
C1
ec- ce De- us no- ster no- bi- scum est,
C2
ec- ce De- us no- ster no- bi- scum est, De- us no- ster et om- ni-
A
ec- ce De- us no- ster no- bi- scum est, De- us no- ster et om- ni-
T
ec- ce De- us no- ster no- bi- scum est,
B
ec- ce De- us no- ster no- bi- scum est, De- us no- - ster et om- ni-
Org.
106
C1
De- us no- ster et om- ni- a, De- us no- ster et om- ni- a, et
C2
-a, ⟨De- us no- ster et om- ni- a,⟩ De- us no- ster et om-
A
-a, De- us no- ster et om-
T
De- us no- - ster et om- ni- a, De- us no- ster, ⟨De- us no- ster⟩
B
-a, De- us no- ster et om- ni- a, De- us no- ster et
Org.

111
C1
C2
A
T
B
Org.
om- ni- a, et om- ni- a, et om- ni- a,
- ni- a, et om- - - ni- a,
- ni- a, et om- - ni- a, ⟨et om- ni- a,⟩ ⟨et
et om- ni- a, et
om- ni- a, et
117
De- us no- ster et om- ni- a.
De- us no- ster et om- ni- a.
om- ni- a,⟩ et om- ni- a, De- us no- ster et om- ni- a.
om- - ni- a, et om- ni- a, De- us no- ster et om- ni- a.
om- - ni- a, et om- ni- a, De- us no- ster et om- ni- a.

18. Justus ut palma

19
C1
ju- stus ut pal- ma flo- re- bit, ⟨ut pal- ma flo-
C2
Ju- stus ut pal- ma flo- re- bit, ut
C3
Ju- stus ut pal- ma flo- re- bit, ut pal- ma flo- re- bit, ⟨ut
A
Ju- - stus ut pal- ma flo- re-
T
Ju- stus ut pal- ma flo- re- bit,
B
Ju- stus ut pal- ma flo- re- bit, ut pal- ma flo-
Org.
4 3 6
23
C1
-re- bit,⟩ sic- ut ce- drus li- ba- ni mul- ti- pli- ca- - bi- tur,
C2
pal- ma flo- re- bit, sic- ut ce- drus li- ba- ni mul- ti- pli- ca- bi- tur,
C3
pal- ma flo- re- bit,⟩ sic- ut ce- drus
A
-bit, sic- ut ce- drus
T
flo- re- bit,
B
-re- bit, sic- ut ce- drus li- ba- ni mul- ti- pli- ca- bi- tur,
Org.
♭ 6 4 3

27
C1
sic- ut ce- drus li- ba- ni in
C2
sic- ut ce- drus li- ba-ni mul- ti- pli- ca- bi- tur
C3
li- ba- ni, ⟨sic- ut ce- drus li- ba- ni⟩ mul- ti- pli- ca- bi- tur in
A
li- ba- ni in
T
sic- ut ce- drus li- ba- ni, ⟨sic- ut ce- drus li- ba- ni⟩ in
B
sic- ut ce- drus li- ba-ni mul- ti- pli- ca- bi- tur in
Org.
♯ ♯ 4 3
31
C1
do- - mo Do- - mi- ni,
C2
in do- mo, in do- mo Do- mi- ni,
C3
do- - mo, in do- mo Do- mi- ni,
A
do- mo, in do- - mo Do- - mi- ni,
T
do- mo, in do- mo, in do- mo Do- mi- ni,
B
do- - - mo Do- mi- ni,
Org.
♭ 4 3

36
C1
ad an- nun- ci- an- dum, ad an- nun- ci- an- - dum ma- ne
C2
ad an- nun- ci- an- - dum, ⟨ad an- nun- ci- an- - dum⟩ ma- ne
C3
ad an- nun- ci- an- - dum, ⟨ad an- nun- ci- an- dum⟩ ma-
Org.
40
mi- se- ri- cor- - di- am tu- am, et ve- ri- ta- tem tu- am,
mi- se- ri- cor- di- am tu- am, et ve- ri- ta- tem tu- am, ⟨et ve- ri- ta- tem
-ne mi- se- ri- cor- di- am tu- am, et ve- ri- ta- tem
44
⟨et ve- ri- ta- tem tu- am,⟩ ⟨et ve- ri- ta- tem tu- am⟩ per noc- tem.
tu- am⟩ per noc- tem, et ve- ri- ta- tem tu- am, ⟨et ve- ri- ta- tem tu- am⟩ per noc- tem.
tu- am per noc- tem, ⟨et ve- ri- ta- tem tu- - am per noc- tem.⟩

49
c3
C1
C2
C3
A
Al- le- lu- ia, al- le- lu- ia, ⟨al- le- lu-
T
Al- le- lu- ia, ⟨al- le- lu- ia,⟩ ⟨al- le- lu-
B
Al- le- lu- ia, al- le- lu- ia, al- -le- lu-
Org.
55
C1
Al- le- lu- ia, al- le- lu- ia, ⟨al- le- lu-
C2
Al- le- lu- ia, al- le- lu- ia, ⟨al- le- lu-
C3
Al- le- lu- ia, ⟨al- le- lu- ia,⟩ ⟨al- le- lu-
A
-ia,⟩
T
-ia,⟩
B
-ia,
Org.

61
C1
-ia,⟩ al- - le- lu- ia, ⟨al- le- lu- ia,⟩
C2
-ia,⟩ ⟨al- le- lu- ia,⟩ ⟨al- le- lu- ia,⟩
C3
-ia,⟩ ⟨al- le- lu- ia,⟩ ⟨al- le- lu- ia,⟩
A
al- le- lu- ia,
T
al- le- lu- ia,
B
al- le- lu- ia,
Org.
5 6 4 3

67
C1
al- - le- lu- ia, al- le- lu- ia.
C2
al- le- lu- ia, ⟨al- - le- lu- ia.⟩
C3
al- le- lu- ia, ⟨al- le- lu- ia.⟩
A
⟨al- le- lu- ia,⟩ ⟨al- le- lu- ia.⟩
T
⟨al- le- lu- ia,⟩ ⟨al- le- lu- ia,⟩ ⟨al- - le- lu- ia.⟩
B
⟨al- le- lu- ia,⟩ ⟨al- le- lu- ia.⟩
Org.
♭ 6 ♯ 6 4 3

72
C1
Be- a- tus vir, ⟨be- a- tus vir,⟩ qui suf-
C2
Be- a- tus vir, ⟨be- a- tus vir,⟩ qui suf-
C3
Be- a- tus vir, be- a- tus vir, qui
A
Be- a- tus vir, qui suf- - fert ten- ta- ti- o- nem, be- a- tus vir,
T
Be- a- tus vir, qui suf- - fert ten- ta- ti- o- nem, be- a- tus vir,
B
Be- a- tus vir, qui suf- fert ten- ta- ti- o- nem, be- a- tus vir,
Org.
77
- fert ten- ta- ti- o- nem, quo- - ni- am
- fert ten- ta- ti- o- nem, quo- - ni- am
suf- fert ten- ta- ti- o- nem, quo- ni- am
quo- ni- am, ⟨quo- ni- am⟩ cum pro- ba- tus
quo- ni- am, quo- ni- am cum pro- ba- tus
quo- ni- am, ⟨quo- ni- am⟩ cum pro- ba- tus

161

87
C1
-et co- ro- - nam vi- tae, co-
C2
-et co- ro- - nam vi- tae, co- ro- - nam vi-
C3
ac- ci- pi- et co- ro- - nam vi-
A
ac- ci- pi- et co- ro- nam,
T
co- ro- nam vi- tae, co- ro-
B
-ci- pi- et co- ro- nam, co- ro- nam vi-
Org.
90
C1
-ro- nam, ac- ci- pi- et co- ro- nam vi- tae, quo- ni- am cum pro- ba-
C2
-tae, co- ro- nam, ac- ci- pi- et co- ro- nam vi- tae,
C3
-tae, ⟨co- ro- nam vi- tae,⟩ ⟨co- ro- nam vi- tae,⟩ quo- ni- am cum pro- ba-
A
co- ro- - nam vi- tae, ⟨co- ro- nam vi- tae,⟩ quo- ni- am cum pro- ba-
T
- nam, co- ro- nam vi- tae, quo- ni- am cum pro- ba-
B
-tae, co- ro- - nam vi- tae, co- ro- nam vi- tae,
Org.

95
C1
-tus fu- e- rit, quo- ni- am, ⟨quo- ni- am⟩ cum pro- ba- tus fu- e- rit,
C2
quo- ni- am, ⟨quo- ni- am⟩ cum pro- ba- tus fu- e- rit, ac- ci- pi-
C3
-tus fu- e- rit, quo- ni- am, ⟨quo- ni- am⟩ cum pro- ba- tus fu- e- rit,
A
-tus fu- e- rit, quo- ni- am, ⟨quo- ni- am⟩ cum pro- ba- tus fu- e- rit, ac-
T
-tus fu- e- rit, quo- ni- am cum pro- ba- tus fu- e- rit,
B
quo- ni- am, ⟨quo- ni- am⟩ cum pro- ba- tus fu- e- rit,
Org.
102
C1
co- ro- nam, ⟨co- ro- nam,⟩
C2
-et co- ro- - nam, ac- ci- pi- et co- ro-
C3
co- ro- nam vi- tae, co- ro-
A
-ci- pi- et co- ro- nam, co- ro- nam vi- tae, co-
T
ac- ci- pi- et co- ro- nam, ac- ci- pi- et co- ro- nam,
B
co- ro- nam vi- tae,
Org.

105
C1
⟨co- ro- nam⟩ vi- tae, co- ro- nam, ac- ci- pi- et, ⟨ac- ci- pi-
C2
- nam vi- tae, co- ro- - nam vi- tae,
C3
- nam, ac- ci- pi- et co- ro- - nam vi- tae, ac- ci- pi-
A
-ro- nam, ⟨co- ro- nam⟩ vi- tae,
T
co- ro- nam vi- tae, ac-
B
ac- ci- pi- et co- ro- nam, ac- ci- pi- et,
Org.
6 4 3 6 4 3

108
C1
-et⟩ co- ro- nam vi- tae, co- ro- nam, co-
C2
ac- ci- pi- et co- ro- nam vi- tae, co- ro- nam,
C3
-et co- ro- nam vi- tae, co- ro- nam vi- tae, co- ro-
A
co- ro- nam, co- ro-
T
-ci- pi- et co- ro- nam vi- tae, ac- ci- pi- et
B
ac- ci- pi- et co- ro- nam vi- tae,
Org.
4 3 6 4 3

Alleluia ut supra [mm. 49–71] si placet

Critical Report

Source

The original 1650 print of Graziani's opus 1 is preserved in three copies, located in: Museo internazionale e biblioteca della musica di Bologna (I-Bc); Biblioteca Casanatense, Rome (I-Rc); and Santini-Bibliothek, Münster (D-MÜs). Only I-Rc has the second soprano partbook.

The opus 1 collection was reprinted in 1652 (in Antwerp) and 1654 (in Rome). Of the 1652 print only the tenor partbook is preserved. The 1654 print only contains thirteen of the eighteen motets in the 1650 original.

Many of the works in this printed collection are also preserved in manuscript copies. These are interesting sources for their own sake, sometimes reflecting local performance traditions, etc., but they are not representative of the composer's intentions.

Therefore, this edition is based on the copy of the original 1650 print owned by I-Bc. The title page reads:

MOTETTI | A DUE, TRE, QUATTRO, | Cinque, e sei voci. | DI D. BONIFATIO | GRATIANI | Maestro di Cappella nella Chiesa del Giesù, | e Seminario Romano. | IN ROMA, Nella Stamperia di Vitale Mascardi. | L'Anno del Giubileo M D C. L. | CON LICENZA DE' SUPERIORI.

Editorial Methods

This edition aims at presenting a critical and authoritative version of the motets from Bonifazio Graziani's opus 1 in a form useful both to scholars and performers.

Part names in the source have been retained but tacitly standardized and are stated at the beginning of each motet. The few tempo and dynamic indications have been retained as in the source. Voicing labels printed in the source, as "Solo," "Cantus primus solus," "A 2," etc., have been reported in the critical notes.

Clefs have been modernized in the edition; the original clefs are shown in the incipit staves. Key signatures have been retained as in the source. Meters have been normalized, employing the sign $\frac{3}{2}$ for a number of variants that in the source signify tripartite meter. Original time signatures are shown in the incipits; also, at changes of meter, if half or more of the active parts have an original signature that differs from the signature shown within the staves of the edition, the original signature is placed above the top staff, with critical notes provided to describe the source readings.

The source is irregularly barred. Single barlines have been tacitly added to the score in accordance with modern conventions. In some cases, this also means that ties have been silently added, stretching over the barline. Double barlines, indicating section breaks, have been retained. The two passages of coloration notation found in "Quid est hoc" are marked by open horizontal brackets above the relevant staves and are mentioned in the critical notes as well.

The original print entirely lacks beaming. In the edition, beams have been added, following the modern convention of beaming according to the time signature. In vocal parts, the beaming follows the syllabic declamation of the text. To make the musical text more easily legible, melismas too are beamed according to the time signature.

All unbroken slurs are original. Such slurs are rare in the source and seem to indicate articulation rather than mere melismas. Slurs added by the editor are dashed. Such editorial slurs have been suggested with great discretion, mostly for parallel passages.

The system of accidentals in the source follows the early modern principle that inflections are valid for the designated note and for repeated notes. This is not altogether consistent in the source, however, and in several cases an inflection appears to be intended for an entire phrase or melisma. The system of accidentals used in the edition follows the modern convention that accidentals remain in effect throughout the measure, but inflections in the source that would be considered redundant according to this modern rule have nonetheless been retained in the edition. This means that inflections called for only by the modern rule are technically editorial, unless made explicit by a source accidental. Editorial inflections that are not indicated by the modern rule are presented within brackets. According to modern conventions, the natural sign is used to cancel inflections where the source uses sharps and flats.

Graziani's motets of opus 1 were composed at a time when a new system of harmonic and tonal organization was about to supplant an older one. Therefore, there are many cases in these works were the decision whether a note should be inflected or not is a choice between the modal melodic line on the one hand, and the harmonic context on the other. In this edition, these critical choices have at most times been made in favor of an interpretation of the harmonic context. At the same time, the musica ficta principles associated with Palestrina's music have still been considered applicable.

The continuo figures in the source have been retained, placed above the organum staff. This includes retaining the source's use of sharps and flats where modern conventions would call for natural signs, despite—as noted above—the use of natural signs in the vocal parts and in the organum's bass line. Clearly erroneous figures have been corrected and reported in the critical notes. Figures within brackets are the editor's additions. Such suggestions have only been added with the utmost discretion. Where the source places a figure to the right of a note, to indicate that the figure reflects a harmonic change taking place after the beat in question, the figure has been placed in the score so that it appears at the point of the corresponding harmonic change. Such editorial realignments most often reflect the voice-leading of the vocal parts. In cases where voice-leading is not evident in the upper parts, the figure has tacitly been aligned to a beat. The performer must, however, note that the placements of figures and resulting harmonic changes are in some cases ambiguous.

Repetitions of the text, in the source marked "ij," are marked with angle brackets. Where there are several such abbreviation marks in a row, the brackets have been repeated, since this generally marks new repetitions of the text.

Critical Notes

The following abbreviations are used in these critical notes: C = Cantus, A = Altus, T = Tenor, B = Bassus, Org. = Organum. Notes are numbered consecutively within a measure. Note values are described using modern terminology (8th note, quarter note, etc.). Pitches are identified using the system in which c' = middle C. The voicing labels noted below have been standardized as "A 2," etc., rather than "à 2," as is sometimes printed in the source.

1. Hic est panis

M. 56, C1, time signature is **3**. M. 71, C2 has "Dominus." M. 78, C1 and C2, time signature is **3**; Org., $\frac{3}{2}$. M. 87, Org., figure $\frac{6}{5}$ is placed to the right of the whole note; in the edition, the figure has been moved to the first beat of m. 88. M. 139, C2, syllable "al-" is under note 2. M. 151, C1 and C2, syllable "al-" is under note 2.

2. Ludite, canite

M. 35, C1, note is dotted whole note. M. 68, C1, note is whole note. M. 69, C1 and Org., voicing label "Solo." M. 94, all parts, voicing label "A 2." M. 120, C2 and Org., voicing label "Solo." M. 137, C1 and Org., voicing label "A 2." M. 146, all parts, voicing label "A 2." M. 172, C1 and Org., voicing label "A 2." M. 209, all parts explicitly have a whole rest at the end of the piece.

3. Omnes gentes

M. 15, C1, note 3, Bologna print has ♯ added in ink. M. 21, Org., note 2, figuring is 4 5. M. 37, C2, time signature is **C**$\frac{3}{2}$; the rest of the parts, $\frac{3}{2}$. Mm. 39–40, Org., placement of single figure ♯ is unclear, possibly intended to align with both note 2 of m. 39 and note 1 of m. 40. M. 68, C1, note 1 is f″, corrected in ink to g″ in the Bologna print. M. 109, C2, note 2 is d″.

4. Amen dico vobis

M. 4, Org., note 1, figure ♯ is ambigously placed between this note and the one before. M. 38, C1 and C2, time signature is **C**$\frac{3}{2}$; Org., $\frac{3}{2}$. M. 55, C1 and C2, time signature is **C**$\frac{3}{2}$; Org., $\frac{3}{2}$.

5. Domine, ne in furore tuo

M. 43, C2 and B, time signature is **3**; the rest, $\frac{3}{2}$. M. 88, Org., note 1, figure 2 placed on last beat of m. 87. M. 105, C1, B, Org., time signature is **3**; C2, $\frac{3}{2}$. M. 110, Org., note 2 is two tied half notes. M. 138, Org., note has figures 4 3.

6. Ad mensam dulcissimi

The Org. part presents the soloistic sections in score notation (vocal part and organ), but without text in the vocal parts. In the edition the vocal partbooks have been used as the primary sources. Discrepancies between the vocal partbooks and the Org. score are specified below.

M. 1, C1 and Org., voicing label "Solo." M. 2, C1, note 7 lacks ♯ in the Org. score. M. 21, C2, voicing label "Solo"; Org., "Canto secondo solo." M. 33, C2 lacks fermata, but fermatas are in the Org. score for both C2 and Org. M. 34, C1 and C2, voicing label "A 2"; Org., "A 2. Canti." M. 59, T, voicing label "Solo"; Org., "Ten. solo." M. 77, C1 and Org., voicing label "Solo." M. 83, C1, time signature is **3**; the rest, $\frac{3}{2}$. M. 83, C1, note 5 explicitly has ♭ in the Org. score. Mm. 83 and 85, C1, no slurs in the Org. score. M. 102, all parts, voicing label "A 3." M. 157, C1, syllable "-vum" is under note 2.

7. Haec est vera fraternitas

M. 12, Org., note 1, figure 2 placed on last beat of m. 11. M. 27, Org., voicing label "B. solo." M. 30, Org., voicing label "2 canti." M. 39, Org., voicing label "A 3."

8. O Jesu, fili Mariae

The Org. part presents the soloistic sections in score notation (vocal part and organ), but without text in the vocal parts. In the edition the vocal partbooks have been used as the primary sources. Discrepancies between the vocal partbooks and the Org. score are specified below.

M. 1, C1, voicing label "Solo"; Org., "Cantus primus solus." M. 7, C1, notes 4–5, no slur in the Org. score. M. 9, Org., in the Bologna print there is a tie in ink between notes 2 and 3. M. 10, C1, notes 4–5 are 8th notes in the Org. score. M. 12, C1, notes 1–2, no tie in the Org. score. M. 14, all parts, voicing label "A 3." M. 42, C3, note is whole note. M. 43, C2, voicing label "Solo"; Org., "Cantus secundus solus." M. 50, C3, voicing label "Solo"; Org., "Cantus tertius solus." M. 51, Org., note is presented as two tied half notes in the source, due to a system break. M. 54, C3, notes 4–5 are 8th notes in the Org. score. M. 58, C3, note 1 is 16th note; the Org. score has 8th note.   Mm. 61–89, in the vocal parts, this section is marked in text as a repeat: "Iesu largitor veniae. ut supra a 3."   M. 89, C3, note is whole note (cf. m. 42).   M. 90, C1, voicing label "Solo"; Org., "Cantus primus solus."   M. 96, C1, notes 1–2 and 5–6 are 8th notes in the Org. score.   M. 103, Org., voicing label "Cantut [sic] secundus solus."   M. 109, C2 and Org., voicing label "A 2."   M. 141, C1, voicing label "Solo"; Org., "Cantus primus solus."   M. 143, C1, notes 2–3, no slur in the Org. score.   M. 146, C1, note 2 lacks ♯ in the Org. score.   M. 153, all parts, voicing label "A 3."   Mm. 164–65, C1, slurs on notes 4–5 of m. 164 and 1–2 of m. 165; in the edition, the slurs have been moved back to notes 2–3 and 4–5 of m. 164.   M. 192, C1, syllable "-ri-" is under note 2.   M. 193, C2 and C3, note is whole note.

9. Aperi mihi

M. 15, B, time signature is 3/2; the rest, **C**3/2.   M. 15, Org., voicing label "A 3."   Mm. 29–30, Org., ambiguous placements of figures in the source.   M. 65, Org., ambiguous placements of figures in the source.

10. Salve, o dulce amoris

M. 1, Org., in this context, *Come stà* might be translated as "Play this precisely as written"; Graziani's intention here is not entirely clear, but arguably it has to do with playing the organum line in the notated octave (i.e., in a high, tenor tessitura), and not in the lower octave.   M. 55, Org., note is whole note.   M. 64, T, note 3 is dotted quarter note.   M. 71, A, note 2 is quarter note.

11. Veni electa mea

M. 18, C3, note is whole note followed by half rest.   M. 27, C1, note 2 has ♯.   M. 41, C2, syllable "me-" is under note 4.   M. 55, C2, note 2 is whole note.   M. 130, C2, tie between notes 1 and 2.

12. Surge, veni

M. 15, T, time signature is 3/2; the rest, **3**.   M. 35, Org., note 3 has figure ♯.   M. 45, C2 and Org., time signature is **3**; T, **C**3/2; C1, 3/2.   M. 103, T, time signature is 3/2; the rest, **3**.   M. 150, T, time signature is 3/2; the rest, **3**.   M. 168, Org. has no double barline.   M. 178, C2, note 4 is b.

13. Rex magne caelitum

M. 24, C1, time signature is **C**3; Org., **3**.   M. 24, C1, voicing label "Solo"; Org., "Canto primo solo."   M. 60, all parts, voicing label "A 3."   M. 71, B, time signature is **C**3/2; the rest, **3**.   M. 86, C2 and Org., time signature is **C**3.   M. 86, C2, voicing label "Solo"; Org., "Canto secondo solo."   M. 89, Org., figures 6 5 are both placed above note 1.   M. 122, C2, B, Org., voicing label "A 3."   M. 138, C1, time signature is **C**3/2; Org., **3**.   M. 138, C1, voicing label "Solo"; Org., "Canto primo solo."   M. 174, C2, time signature is **C**3/2; B, 3/2; Org., **3**.   M. 174, all parts, voicing label "A 3."

14. Anima nostra

M. 13, C2 and T, time signature is **3**; B and Org., 3/2.   M. 25, Org., voicing label "Solo."   M. 30, Org., figures 4 3 are both placed above note 1.   M. 41, Org., time signature is **3**.   M. 61, C1, B, Org., voicing label "A 4"; C2, "A 3."   M. 69, B, no rest at the beginning of the measure.   M. 148, C2, note is longa.

15. Quid est hoc

M. 1, C1, voicing label "Solo"; Org., "Canto solo."   M. 10, Org., voicing label "Bas[so]."   M. 16, Org., voicing label "Canto."   M. 41, C1, notes 3–4 are e♭"–d".   M. 47, Org., voicing label "Canto solo."   Mm. 47–71, B, twenty-six measures of rest indicated, rather than twenty-five.   Mm. 51–54, C1, notated in ¢ with black hemiola notation.   Mm. 64–67, C1, C2, A, notated in ¢ with black hemiola notation.   M. 97, C1, time signature is 3/2; the rest, **C**3/2.   M. 123, Org., figures 4 3 are both placed above note 1.   M. 138, A, note 5 is e'.   M. 153, A, note 6 is b♭.   M. 156, A, note 1 is a.

16. O principes

M. 10, Org., note 3, figure is ♭7.   M. 50, C1, C2, note is dotted whole note; time signature (¢) is placed at beginning of m. 51.   M. 66, T, B, Org., voicing label "A 3."   M. 100, C1, C2, Org., voicing label "A 2."   M. 105, A, T, B, Org., voicing label "A 3."   M. 109, C1, C2, Org., voicing label "A 2."   M. 116, C1, C2, A, T, Org., voicing label "A 5."   M. 121, A, time signature is 3/2; the rest, **3**.   M. 133, A, T, B, note is dotted whole note; time signature (¢) is placed at beginning of m. 134.   M. 134, Org., voicing label "A 3."   M. 135, Org., voicing label "A 2."   M. 137, T, time signature is 3/2; the rest, **3**.   M. 137, Org., voicing label "A 3."   M. 139, Org., voicing label "A 2."   M. 143, Org., voicing label "A 5."   M. 149, C2, A, T, note is dotted whole note; time signature (¢) is placed at beginning of m. 150.   Mm. 157–58, C1, syllables "co-ro-" are under m. 157, note 6, and m. 158, note 1, respectively.   M. 159, B, syllables "co-ro-" are under note 4 and note 5, respectively.   M. 163, T, time signature is 3/2; the rest, **3**.   M. 171, T, note is dotted whole note.   M. 176, C1, note 1 is g♭" and note 2 is e" (the ♭ is obviously misplaced).   M. 179, C1, C2, A, B, note is dotted whole note; time signature (¢) is placed at beginning of m. 180.

17. Venite gentes

M. 1, C1, voicing label "Solo."   M. 16, C2 and Org., time signature is 3/2; the rest, **C**3/2.   M. 16, C1, T, Org., voicing label "A 5."   M. 16, Org., extra pitch A, apparently with value of whole note, crossed out in ink in the Bologna print.   M. 29, C1 has "gentes" under notes 1–2.   M. 65, C1, time signature is **3**; the rest, 3/2.   Mm. 71–72, C1, C2, notated with black hemiola notation.   Mm. 79–80, C1, C2, notated with black hemiola notation.   Mm. 96–97, C1, notated with black hemiola notation.   M. 105, Org., note 1, figure is 6/4.   M. 112, C1, T, B, time signature is **3**; the rest, 3/2.   M. 123, C1, T, B, note is whole note.

18. Justus ut palma

M. 1, C1, voicing label "Solo"; Org., "Canto p° solo."   M. 4, Org., one note is missing here, most likely a whole note on pitch c (ink markings in m. 7 of the Bologna print are apparently traces of an attempt to solve the resulting problems).   M. 19, C1 and Org., voicing label "A 6."   M. 36, C1, C2, voicing label "A 3"; Org., "A 3. Can[ti]."   M. 49, C1, time signature is $\mathbf{C}^3_2$; Org., **3**; the rest, $\mathbf{C3}$.   M. 49, Org., voicing label "A 3."   M. 72, Org., voicing label "A 6."   M. 73, Org., note 2, figure is ♭6.   M. 84, C2, notes 13–14 are f"–e".   M. 86, T, syllable "-nam" is under note 6.   M. 113, A, note 1, syllable "-tae" is missing.   M. 93, T and B, time signature is $\frac{3}{2}$; the rest, **3**.   M. 114, C2, note is dotted whole note.

Recent Researches in the Music of the Baroque Era
Steven Saunders, general editor

Vol.	Composer: Title
1	Marc-Antoine Charpentier: *Judicium Salomonis*
2	Georg Philipp Telemann: *Forty-eight Chorale Preludes*
3	Johann Caspar Kerll: *Missa Superba*
4–5	Jean-Marie Leclair: *Sonatas for Violin and Basso continuo, Opus 5*
6	*Ten Eighteenth-Century Voluntaries*
7–8	William Boyce: *Two Anthems for the Georgian Court*
9	Giulio Caccini: *Le nuove musiche*
10–11	Jean-Marie Leclair: *Sonatas for Violin and Basso continuo, Opus 9 and Opus 15*
12	Johann Ernst Eberlin: *Te Deum; Dixit Dominus; Magnificat*
13	Gregor Aichinger: *Cantiones Ecclesiasticae*
14–15	Giovanni Legrenzi: *Cantatas and Canzonets for Solo Voice*
16	Giovanni Francesco Anerio and Francesco Soriano: *Two Settings of Palestrina's "Missa Papae Marcelli"*
17	Giovanni Paolo Colonna: *Messe a nove voci concertata con stromenti*
18	Michel Corrette: *"Premier livre d'orgue" and "Nouveau livre de noëls"*
19	Maurice Greene: *Voluntaries and Suites for Organ and Harpsichord*
20	Giovanni Antonio Piani: *Sonatas for Violin Solo and Violoncello with Cembalo*
21–22	Marin Marais: *Six Suites for Viol and Thoroughbass*
23–24	Dario Castello: *Selected Ensemble Sonatas*
25	*A Neapolitan Festa a Ballo and Selected Instrumental Ensemble Pieces*
26	Antonio Vivaldi: *The Manchester Violin Sonatas*
27	Louis-Nicolas Clérambault: *Two Cantatas for Soprano and Chamber Ensemble*
28	Giulio Caccini: *Nuove musiche e nuova maniera di scriverle (1614)*
29–30	Michel Pignolet de Montéclair: *Cantatas for One and Two Voices*
31	Tomaso Albinoni: *Twelve Cantatas, Opus 4*
32–33	Antonio Vivaldi: *Cantatas for Solo Voice*
34	Johann Kuhnau: *Magnificat*
35	Johann Stadlmayr: *Selected Magnificats*
36–37	Jacopo Peri: *Euridice: An Opera in One Act, Five Scenes*
38	Francesco Severi: *Salmi passaggiati (1615)*
39	George Frideric Handel: *Six Concertos for the Harpsichord or Organ (Walsh's Transcriptions, 1738)*
40	*The Brasov Tablature (Brasov Music Manuscript 808): German Keyboard Studies 1608–1684*
41	John Coprario: *Twelve Fantasias for Two Bass Viols and Organ and Eleven Pieces for Three Lyra Viols*

42	Antonio Cesti: *Il pomo d'oro (Music for Acts III and V from Modena, Biblioteca Estense, Ms. Mus. E. 120)*
43	Tomaso Albinoni: *Pimpinone: Intermezzi comici musicali*
44–45	Antonio Lotti: *Duetti, terzetti, e madrigali a piu voci*
46	Matthias Weckmann: *Four Sacred Concertos*
47	Jean Gilles: *Requiem (Messe des morts)*
48	Marc-Antoine Charpentier: *Vocal Chamber Music*
49	*Spanish Art Song in the Seventeenth Century*
50	Jacopo Peri: *"Le varie musiche" and Other Songs*
51–52	Tomaso Albinoni: *Sonatas and Suites, Opus 8, for Two Violins, Violoncello, and Basso continuo*
53	Agostino Steffani: *Twelve Chamber Duets*
54–55	Gregor Aichinger: *The Vocal Concertos*
56	Giovanni Battista Draghi: *Harpsichord Music*
57	*Concerted Sacred Music of the Bologna School*
58	Jean-Marie Leclair: *Sonatas for Violin and Basso continuo, Opus 2*
59	Isabella Leonarda: *Selected Compositions*
60–61	Johann Schelle: *Six Chorale Cantatas*
62	Denis Gaultier: *La Rhétorique des Dieux*
63	Marc-Antoine Charpentier: *Music for Molière's Comedies*
64–65	Georg Philipp Telemann: *Don Quichotte auf der Hochzeit des Comacho: Comic Opera-Serenata in One Act*
66	Henry Butler: *Collected Works*
67–68	John Jenkins: *The Lyra Viol Consorts*
69	*Keyboard Transcriptions from the Bach Circle*
70	Melchior Franck: *Geistliche Gesäng und Melodeyen*
71	Georg Philipp Telemann: *Douze solos, à violon ou traversière*
72	Marc-Antoine Charpentier: *Nine Settings of the "Litanies de la Vierge"*
73	*The Motets of Jacob Praetorius II*
74	Giovanni Porta: *Selected Sacred Music from the Ospedale della Pietà*
75	*Fourteen Motets from the Court of Ferdinand II of Hapsburg*
76	Jean-Marie Leclair: *Sonatas for Violin and Basso continuo, Opus 1*
77	Antonio Bononcini: *Complete Sonatas for Violoncello and Basso continuo*
78	Christoph Graupner: *Concerti Grossi for Two Violins*
79	Paolo Quagliati: *Il primo libro de' madrigali a quattro voci*
80	Melchior Franck: *Dulces Mundani Exilij Deliciae*
81	*Late-Seventeenth-Century English Keyboard Music*
82	*Solo Compositions for Violin and Viola da gamba with Basso continuo*
83	Barbara Strozzi: *Cantate, ariete a una, due e tre voci, Opus 3*
84	Charles-Hubert Gervais: *Super flumina Babilonis*
85	Henry Aldrich: *Selected Anthems and Motet Recompositions*

86	Lodovico Grossi da Viadana: *Salmi a quattro cori*
87	Chiara Margarita Cozzolani: *Motets*
88	Elisabeth-Claude Jacquet de La Guerre: *Cephale et Procris*
89	Sébastien Le Camus: *Airs à deux et trois parties*
90	Thomas Ford: *Lyra Viol Duets*
91	*Dedication Service for St. Gertrude's Chapel, Hamburg, 1607*
92	Johann Klemm: *Partitura seu Tabulatura italica*
93	Giovanni Battista Somis: *Sonatas for Violin and Basso continuo, Opus 3*
94	John Weldon: *The Judgment of Paris*
95–96	Juan Bautista Comes: *Masses. Parts 1–2*
97	Sebastian Knüpfer: *Lustige Madrigalien und Canzonetten*
98	Stefano Landi: *La morte d'Orfeo*
99	Giovanni Battista Fontana: *Sonatas for One, Two, and Three Parts with Basso continuo*
100	Georg Philipp Telemann: *Twelve Trios*
101	Fortunato Chelleri: *Keyboard Music*
102	Johann David Heinichen: *La gara degli Dei*
103	Johann David Heinichen: *Diana su l'Elba*
104	Alessandro Scarlatti: *Venere, Amore e Ragione*
105	*Songs with Theorbo (ca. 1650–1663)*
106	Melchior Franck: *Paradisus Musicus*
107	Heinrich Ignaz Franz von Biber: *Missa Christi resurgentis*
108	Johann Ludwig Bach: *Motets*
109–10	Giovanni Rovetta: *Messa, e salmi concertati, op. 4 (1639). Parts 1–2*
111	Johann Joachim Quantz: *Seven Trio Sonatas*
112	*Petits motets from the Royal Convent School at Saint Cyr*
113	Isabella Leonarda: *Twelve Sonatas, Opus 16*
114	Rudolph di Lasso: *Virginalia Eucharistica (1615)*
115	Giuseppe Torelli: *Concerti musicali, Opus 6*
116–17	Nicola Francesco Haym: *Complete Sonatas. Parts 1–2*
118	Benedetto Marcello: *Il pianto e il riso delle quattro stagioni*
119	Loreto Vittori: *La Galatea*
120–23	William Lawes: *Collected Vocal Music. Parts 1–4*
124	Marco da Gagliano: *Madrigals. Part 1*
125	Johann Schop: *Erster Theil newer Paduanen*
126	Giovanni Felice Sances: *Motetti a una, due, tre, e quattro voci (1638)*
127	Thomas Elsbeth: *Sontägliche Evangelien*
128–30	Giovanni Antonio Rigatti: *Messa e salmi, parte concertati. Parts 1–3*
131	*Seventeenth-Century Lutheran Church Music with Trombones*
132	Francesco Cavalli: *La Doriclea*

133	*Music for "Macbeth"*
134	Domenico Allegri: *Music for an Academic Defense (Rome, 1617)*
135	Jean Gilles: *Diligam te, Domine*
136	Silvius Leopold Weiss: *Lute Concerti*
137	*Masses by Alessandro Scarlatti and Francesco Gasparini*
138	Giovanni Ghizzolo: *Madrigali et arie per sonare et cantare*
139	Michel Lambert: *Airs from "Airs de différents autheurs"*
140	William Babell: *Twelve Solos for a Violin or Oboe with Basso Continuo. Book 1*
141	Giovanni Francesco Anerio: *Selva armonica (Rome, 1617)*
142–43	Bellerofonte Castaldi: *Capricci (1622). Parts 1–2*
144	Georg von Bertouch: *Sonatas a 3*
145	Marco da Gagliano: *Madrigals. Part 2*
146	Giovanni Rovetta: *Masses*
147	Giacomo Antonio Perti: *Five-Voice Motets for the Assumption of the Virgin Mary*
148	Giovanni Felice Sances: *Motetti a 2, 3, 4, e cinque voci (1642)*
149	*La grand-mére amoureuse, parodie d'Atys*
150	Andreas Hammerschmidt: *Geistlicher Dialogen Ander Theil*
151	Georg von Bertouch: *Three Sacred Cantatas*
152	Giovanni Maria Ruggieri: *Two Settings of the Gloria*
153	Alessandro Scarlatti: *Concerti sacri, opera seconda*
154	Johann Sigismund Kusser: *Adonis*
155	John Blow: *Selected Verse Anthems*
156	Anton Holzner: *Viretum pierium (1621)*
157	Alessandro Scarlatti: *Venere, Adone, et Amore*
158	Marc-Antoine Charpentier: *In nativitatem Domini canticum, H. 416*
159	Francesco Scarlatti: *Six Concerti Grossi*
160	Charles Avison: *Concerto Grosso Arrangements of Geminiani's Opus 1 Violin Sonatas*
161	Johann David Heinichen: *Selected Music for Vespers*
162–63	Francesco Gasparini: *Cantatas with Violins. Parts 1–2*
164–65	Antoine Boesset: *Sacred Music. Parts 1–2*
166	Andreas Hammerschmidt: *Selections from the "Gespräche" (1655–56) with Capellen*
167	Santiago de Murcia: *Cifras selectas de guitarra*
168	Gottfried Heinrich Stölzel: *German Te Deum*
169	Biagio Marini: *Compositioni varie per musica di camera, Opus 13*
170	Santiago Billoni: *Complete Works*
171	Marco da Gagliano: *La Flora*
172	Girolamo Polani: *Six Chamber Cantatas for Solo Voice*
173	Bonifazio Graziani: *Motets for Two to Six Voices, Opus 1*